The Journey Within

*How to create
the dynamic of recovery to transform your habits
and become your authentic self*

Written by

Wanda Webster & Christopher Mack

The Journey Within

www.dynamicsofrecovery.com

info@dynamicsofrecovery.com

This book is dedicated to John Jefferson, who labored in the field of recovery in the Skid Row district of Los Angeles for many years. He was affectionately known as J.J. He inspired us into a life of service and the eventual writing of this book. We love you and miss you dearly.

The 15 Year War

no bullets
no guns
no bombs
no blood
15 years at war with myself

no boots
no kevlar
no helmet
no pistol
15 years at war with myself

who has won the battles I've fought?
so often stalemate
(always attrition)
how many casualties?
how much harm?

the war is over.
it's calm now.
waves of peace.
an armistice with myself

negotiations were tough
each side entrenched
there was no victor.
but an uneasy quiet sits over the battlefield in my soul

the few pockets of resistance have been quelled.
the field smokes
and will always remind me of this conflict.
but it is over
i have come home
after,
15 years at war with myself

mark wilkins 2019

Table of Contents

INTRODUCTION

This book explores ideas, attitudes, and behaviors that keep us trapped and in bondage to ourselves. It brings an understanding of individual patterns that keep us from being the best possible version of ourselves. We invite you to walk down the dark halls of your mind to find out who you really are. To cause this profound transformation of your being, it requires in-depth exploration, keen self-observation, and finally, an integration of every aspect of yourself. You only need to be willing to face yourself. Are you ready to be fully authentic and more magnificent than anything you ever imagined?

Note:
Some people have been too traumatized to attempt their healing process by themselves. If this is you, please seek the assistance of a clinical psychologist or similar professional to guide you through to the other side. This additional support system of experienced individuals is necessary to ensure that you healthily process your trauma and wounds with no adverse side effects.

**God might be a distorted or disastrous idea in the individual. So we refer to guidance from Source, from the Divine or the Light. Use whatever terminology works for you. The name is not as crucial as your process to connect to a higher power, your inner guidance, and your Higher Self.

PREFACE

This book was born from a 10-week program based upon the works of Dr. Carl Gustav Jung, the big book of Alcoholics Anonymous, and upon the observations and shared experiences from participants in our programs. All paragraphs in italics are direct dialogue from participants and kept anonymous out of respect for them.

Hopefully, this book will create the dynamic of recovery within you the reader so that you are better able to accept all aspects and dimensions of yourself. We wrote this book because we believe the greatest tragedy of all is living a life disconnected from our authentic selves. When we move forward in life through our pain and our darkness, we will transform as we learn more about who we really are. When we know and accept ourselves, we learn to love ourselves and others more. Accepting ourselves, our situation, and our dark side is the key to our own transformation. Then we are creating a life of deeper connection to all living things, and to the Divine nature of the universe.

We have seen that knowledge by itself does not change anything, so we created a journal section with questions for the reader's own investigation. We strongly encourage daily meditation too. We know that we must go more in-depth into long lost events and feelings to transform them. The way out is to go within because everything outside of ourselves has the potential to create an addiction. The last frontier is inside of ourselves. We believe we each have all the answers we ever need within us. Your greatest gift to the world is your own self-realization.

CHAPTER ONE

It's More Than A Flesh Wound

It is incredible how films show fist fights or bar room brawls where the lead character or protagonist can walk away with barely a limp. Our hero (male or female) usually swaggers triumphantly away with minimal visible signs of injury. We even believe it to be realistic; we too could 'just walk it off' when we are hurt and bleeding. The filmmakers need us to believe in invincible heroes, but life does not work this way.

We have all endured a physical wound at some point in our lives. We even know how best to treat most of these physical wounds. If they are not cleaned or bandaged, the injuries can become infected, and then they become more difficult to heal. They fester and become red and swollen, and the pain increases. It is like the body is sending out signals for us to please pay attention and give some tender loving care to it. If we do not, the damage can be irreparable.

But what about our internal wounds and traumas? Has anyone ever taught you how to take care of those? We all have them. We cannot escape from life without some internal wounds too. And if we do not heal our inner wounds, they also fester and become worse over time. They start sending out messages to our brain that are based on a perception of when the injury occurred. But if that wound happened five years ago, or even thirty years ago, more than likely, today it is based on a misperception and untruth.

Let's say that you had some pretty great parents. They loved you and never abused you. But, what if every time your father came home, he picked up your little brother first? You might think, 'He loves my little brother more than me.' That hurts. That becomes a wound, and it becomes more infected every time your father does it. And your father has no idea he is hurting you; he is just doing something that seems natural and reasonable to him. But children take things very personally because they don't have the emotional maturity to do otherwise.

Now, can you see how we might receive hundreds of wounds and traumas as children? It has even been hypothesized that babies can feel their mother's pain and unhappiness while in the womb. Some of the more damaging and apparent wounds are sexual abuse, physical abuse, bullying at school, emotional abuse like intense criticism and neglect, divorce, or death. Most if not every one of us has experienced at least one severe trauma as a child between the ages of 0-6 years old. This original wound often then becomes a recurrent theme in your life.

When I was around four years old, my uncle inappropriately touched me. I was confused and told my mother what happened. I could tell she was distraught, but I was not comforted and reassured. I kept waiting for my parents to talk to me about it, but nothing happened. My uncle left the house, but I felt terrible like I had done something wrong. For years after, I never fully trusted my parents. They had let me down; not being the supportive or protective parent in an abusive situation. I felt I had to be the strong one, do the parenting, do everything, never depend on anyone for anything. 'I don't need you,' became my protective mantra. Consequently, I had many failed relationships based on this erroneous belief over the years.

When we tell ourselves, we don't need other people, we build a wall around ourselves and cannot become vulnerable and open to expressing and receiving love. Having a deep and intimate relationship becomes impossible if our fears or wounds are running our life. We have the basic need as human beings to feel connected to others and to be seen and heard. If we are proclaiming otherwise, we are not being honest with ourselves. We are not being authentic.

If we want to heal ourselves, we must look deeply at our wounds. We must go through the pain in order to fully recover. We cannot go around our hurts or compartmentalize these wounds and ignore them any longer. They are festering inside of us, and it becomes harder and harder the longer we ignore the signals they are sending to us. Just like a physical wound becomes more difficult to heal if you ignore it, so too do the internal wounds. If you have significant reactions to many things in your life, to many situations and people, then it is a good indication that your wounds are running your life, not you. If you are in pain, you will profoundly react to others in many different types of situations.

Your feelings, attitudes, and behaviors change because of your wounds. If you are operating out of your injuries, it is impossible to have a healthy life. If you are living out of past wounds most of the time, you do not see how those can take control of your life. You are instead kidnapped, held hostage by duct tape, and you did it to yourself! There is no ransom for the kidnapping, who do you pay!?

My mom and dad separated, and my stepdad was abusive to all of us. I only remember going to court and being separated and being sent to a foster home. They were nice and bought us presents. When we went back to court, my mother got custody, but I realized I blamed my mother for the abuse. My relationships with all women were horrible because of my resentment with my mother.

Sometimes it becomes tough to find the entry point of some of your wounds because they are so buried or hidden so deep. We might not have any knowledge of what has hurt us and what keeps hurting us. Resentment is the number one indicator that you have a culprit on the scene. It means you are carrying the hurt long after the incident. Resentments are like picking at the scab on a wound, it becomes annoying and keeps it from healing. You keep picking the scab because you don't understand the hurt and you keep reacting to life.

We all have the same needs as children. We need food, clothing, and shelter. We require protection and security; a need for honesty, fairness, and keeping agreements. We have a need to express our unique creativity and to feel that we belong and are valued. We need affection, companionship, and kindness from others. We need to play and have fun while experiencing connection and support. We need acknowledgment, appreciation, and challenges. We need autonomy, freedom, and to make our own choices. We need understanding and empathy. We need peace, love, and we even have a need to help others.

When your emotional and physical needs are met, you want to BECOME MORE. When your needs are not met, you just WANT MORE.

3

Your wounds cause you to want things like food, approval, love, drugs, alcohol, material things, money, or sex. But none of these things quench your thirst for more and more. You keep trying to fill your wound, but it is unfillable because you are filling it with the wrong stuff. The hole gets bigger and bigger because you have not addressed the issue. You use things to identify with like your clothes, your car, your cell phone, your job, and even your crack pipe! Congratulations! You are now under the influence of unconsciousness.

When I was four years old, I walked in on my mom, and she was smoking a crack pipe with her boyfriend. I knew whatever she was doing was wrong. Shortly afterward, my brother and I were put into foster homes. I don't even know how I feel now, but I am one hundred pounds overweight, and I have an addiction to drugs. I now see how these things are related to my mom and my childhood. I see how I am trying to fill myself up with food, so I don't hurt anymore.

Many of us go through life and never examine ourselves. We are so distracted by our social media, sport's teams, families, jobs, and television, that we have little extra time to devote to introspection. And why go to the 'bad stuff' so that we have to feel those terrible feelings again and again? Once was bad enough! We think it is over and, in the past, so why bother? But when we become conscious of the wound, we have the ammunition to heal it. The scars are blocking us from becoming our best version of ourselves.

We must go through the pain, not ignore it or try to hide it away in a compartment we have created. We must learn how to embrace all of our imperfections, wounds, and traumas to get to a better place, to find that elusive peace inside. To become a better human being. To stop being a victim. To stop being so needy. To stop feeling entitled to things we have not earned. The secrets are our wounds, constantly inputting jagged information into our minds. The wounds make us bad people to ourselves. We make low-grade decisions based on low grade hurts we feel. In the beginning, we make excuses for bad behavior. We are like a big walking sore, created by something that happened when we were a kid.

When I thought about the trauma, the chemistry in my body started changing. But when I went through it and started speaking about the positive aspects, I felt another shift in my chemistry. I felt lighter as the burdens began lifting. I finally realized that my consciousness expanded the more I healed my past!

The getting high is a by-product or side effect of the wounds, just like the overeating, the gambling, or whatever substance is your choice. We just want to feel good; to feel some sort of relief. We have a compulsion to feel better, but it disconnects us from our wounds and our authentic selves. Remember the Incredible Hulk? He was searching for something to cure his wound or heal himself. But he always ran into someone who magnified his flaw, someone who made him turn into the Hulk. You too will become reactive towards life and people if you do not heal those wounds inside of you.

One of the reasons we do not like to look at our lives more closely is because then we might be faced with making a change. Human beings do not like change. It makes us feel uncomfortable, scared, nervous, tired, and even angry. Our resistance comes out, and we push back with rationalizations and defense strategies on why the change is not necessary. Often, we resist the change until the pain of not changing becomes greater than the pain of change.

If you look at the stories in films, they mirror human nature. There is a reason for this; we can more easily relate to the stories being told. The main character, the hero, or protagonist of a film, has a journey he must take. He never takes on this journey with joy and excitement; he first shows his resistance. (Just like we do) After the first 30 pages or so in the script, the hero is propelled into his new journey by an extreme event. We love seeing the resistance in our hero because we do the same thing in our lives. We resist change, even when we know it is good for us.

Your resistance might look like this: "I already know the answer." "I can handle this." "No one can tell me what to do!" "It's not my fault." "He/she started it." "I will start it tomorrow." "I don't know how; I can't do it." "I don't need anyone else." "This doesn't make sense to me." "I have something more important to do." "This sounds crazy." Your resistance might be a personal attack on another person. You blame them, you call them names or you make fun of them/it. And then you justify and rationalize why things are OK just the way they are. The mind can have very clever thoughts and ideas, but these ideas and thoughts never seem to work out as you imagine.

When I was four years old, my mother called the police on my father and had him taken out of the house. He was not doing anything to warrant this action, he was just getting ready to take a bath. I remember sitting on the couch and crying so hard that I could not breathe. I loved my father so much; the pain of this traumatic event was almost too much for me to handle. For years I hated the police and did not have a great relationship with my mother. By the time I was 18 years old, every time I saw the cops, I would fight them. I remember saying to myself, 'You can't make me do anything!' I never saw the connection to these events until I started asking myself questions like, 'Why don't I have a great relationship with my mother?' I blamed her for taking my father away. I rebelled against the police even when I had done nothing wrong. I was setting myself up for suicide by another's hands because my pain was running my life and making decisions for me.

Do you ever wake up in pain and not know why? That pain is in your emotional body. It will take an examination to get a diagnosis. Your prognosis is dependent upon your ability to treat what has happened to you. We just keep trying to fill our wounds, but they are unfillable. We are trying to fill them with the wrong stuff. The hole keeps getting bigger because we have never addressed the real issue.

Once the wound is healed, our lives start to transform and change. We become free and authentic to be who we really are on a deep soul level. But we must first identify where the resistance is showing up to break free of what is holding us back. Imagine being open and humble and grateful......that would be the opposite to resisting others and life. If you are not there, some wounds need to be investigated and healed. You cannot transform your life if you are running away from your hurts.

Every hero in a film goes through a transformation. By the end of the film, he/she can do something new, something that he was unable to do at the beginning of the film or story. All of us go through small transformations and hopefully significant changes throughout our lives. It is because of our wounds that we resist this journey of transformation. We are too wounded to live life fully, to take chances, to embrace change, and to let go of our fears.

Remember Luke Skywalker in Star Wars? He was reluctant to leave home and put up a lot of resistance to starting on his journey to believing in himself and taking ownership of his power. It is only when his parents die that he must leave; he is given no other choice. Again, we love seeing this resistance because we can relate to it. It reminds us of ourselves, and we can look at his character without harsh judgment (perhaps unlike looking at ourselves).

The main character, Rick, in Casablanca (played by Humphrey Bogart) runs the most popular nightspot. But he is cynical and just wants to be left alone. He is resistant to take a stand to defend truth and justice. When his ex-lover, Ilsa, (Ingrid Bergman) appears we understand why he is so bitter and unhappy. His resistance only becomes more pronounced. We the audience can relate because we have all been hurt by someone too. We know what that bitterness feels like and how it can affect our future decisions and relationships.

It is easy to see the resistance in characters in films and other people around us. It is so obvious where they are in denial and how they need to push through their pain and get through to the other side. Why is it so difficult to see our resistance? Because we are not used to turning our observations back to ourselves. We focus so much on what others are doing or not doing that we don't have time to look within and see what snags us in life. It feels better to see what is wrong with others than to admit what is wrong with us.

And that is precisely the point. If we feel too ashamed to look at our wounds and flaws, then it means we have been wounded a lot. Even the best-intentioned parents caused us emotional pain and injuries. School was very painful for most of us because kids can be the cruelest to each other. We have all said and done things as children that we would not think of doing as adults. Or maybe you were the unfortunate one that was bullied by others. We see kids today committing suicide because this pain is too much for them to handle.

We feel less than because of our wounds and traumas. We feel ashamed because an adult sexually molested us, an innocent child. We think we cannot do the same things that others can because of all the criticism we received from a well-meaning adult or perhaps a damaged adult. We assume that love hurts because of how we were treated. We feel hurt and afraid of life because life always felt unfair to us. We are angry that life does not work out as we want it to, and we cannot figure out how to fix it. We are frustrated and give up on many dreams because what is the point?

All I remember is that I was always criticized by my mother. I could not do anything right in her eyes. I had 10 brothers and sisters, and I had to take care of them a lot. But it always ended badly; they would tell my mother something that I supposedly did wrong, and I would get into trouble. Her criticisms would cut me like a knife. I tried to defend myself, but she would not listen to me. I became very depressed and ran away from home. For many years I could not hear any feedback or critique without going into a tailspin with my emotions. Every time it took me back to the injustice I felt with my mother's criticisms.

We can have freedom from our emotional, mental, and physical pain, instead of feeling imprisoned by them. It starts by looking at our wounds with sincere honesty and acceptance. You cannot change something that you are not aware of. Awareness is the very first step to releasing the emotional pain of the past. Know that it was not your fault, no matter what happened to you. But, it is your responsibility to create a better life now, to do something about it. We think nothing about dressing a physical wound, know it needs to be done. But most of us are utterly unsure of how to heal our inner wounds. You were just never taught how to do it, how to treat an emotional wound.

Journaling is a great tool to help you clearly see how you were wounded. By writing down the situation and incident, and then expressing how it made you feel, creates a small release. You are actually going through the pain instead of compartmentalizing it or pushing it away, hoping never to feel it again. There will be resistance toward journaling, embrace the resistance too. Write about the opposition, ask yourself, "Why do I feel so much resistance?" See how answering that question will, in fact, dissolve a lot of your resistance.

While journaling, some of your insecurities, fears, and limitations will come out. This is a part of the process. They are just feelings. There has been a cover-up for years, and you must feel it to heal it. Know that there are no perfect people, perfection does not exist. If it did, we would have no place to grow and transform, and that would become very boring. Every character in a film also has what we call character flaws, areas that are not perfect within. Otherwise, he/she would have no transformation to undergo.

Can you imagine going to watch a film with a perfect main character? This person is perfect at the beginning of the film, and perfect at the end - no change whatsoever. We would become very bored watching this story, and think, 'What is the point of this film?' We would not be able to relate to the story because we are not perfect. We would not have any emotional release because our hero did not go through any transformation or growth (his emotional release).

If you don't acknowledge your weaknesses, they capture you in the most unexpected times. If you recognize your flaws, guilt and shame cannot come knocking at your door trying to sell you something. When you start having a personal relationship with yourself, there will be no need to justify and rationalize anything about yourself. Journaling will help you realize your strengths, your weaknesses, and your limitations. Justifying and rationalizing will just keep you in a slump.

Jung understood this deeply, and this is why Alan Watts said:

> [Jung] *was the sort of man who could feel anxious and afraid and guilty without being ashamed of feeling this way.* **In other words, he understood that an integrated person is not a person who has simply eliminated the sense of guilt or the sense of anxiety from his life – who is fearless and wooden and kind of sage of stone. He is a person who feels all these things, but has no recriminations against himself for feeling them.**

Sometimes you might be aware that you want to change but are unsure exactly how to do it. You have been waking up in pain for a long time. You might blindly look for a way out, for other avenues to take, for an alternative choice, but find yourself rationalizing that things are not so bad. You give yourself cues that it could be worse! You justify that life is not perfect, so it is OK to stay in a relationship that isn't working, an unfulfilling job, or within an abusive family situation.

Paramahansa Yogananda said that all religion is based on the attainment of pleasure and the avoidance of pain. This is what humans do over and over, causing bad habits that are not easy to break. Our addiction to pleasure is distracting and destructive. And the world of drugs and drinking can be hard and dangerous work. The pleasure gotten from the high does not last long, and the journey to secure more can involve a dangerous road. It isn't fun to have someone pull a knife on you at three in the morning and steal your money to buy more drugs. This is an extreme example of avoiding our pain in lieu of pleasure. Have you ever asked yourself, "Why do I always have to feel good?"

But the only way to really get rid of our pain and suffering is to bring it into the Light, bring our complete awareness to what initially caused our traumas and wounds from childhood. Investigate your attitudes, perceptions, and beliefs because of your wounds. How did they change you as a child? As an adult? Are there resentments and anger that surface throughout your days and weeks? Are you secretive about your past? Does your life feel like it is out of control and unmanageable? Is your makeup smeared with self-pity? Do you blame others for your circumstances? Are you discontented, restless, irritable, and full of fear?

If you have considerable resistance to change and authority figures, you are not willing to let go of your self-centeredness to bring a positive transformation into your life. Your best thinking got you where you are today, are you happy with it? Or do you desire something better? Your ego will want to keep things a certain way, wanting what it wants when it wants it. It will take a spiritual experience to heal you and to awaken your true potential. Dr. Carl Jung explained spiritual experiences as vital phenomena that appear to be in the nature of huge emotional displacements and rearrangements. It is when your ideas, emotions, and attitudes which were once guiding forces are suddenly cast to one side, and a completely new set of conceptions and motives begin to dominate you.

My father unexpectedly died when I was only 4 years old. It seemed that everything changed for the worse after that. We had to move, we became poor, my mother was unhappy and cried all the time, and I felt utterly abandoned. I now realize this event negatively affected my life for years. I could never fill the deep hole inside of me, longing for a relationship, but they never worked out and drinking too much to avoid the grief and pain. I could never let go of the story of "What if?" What if my father had never died? What if I had a loving relationship with my father today?

Socrates, the ancient Greek philosopher, famously stated that an unexamined life was not worth living. When we examine ourselves, we gain a better understanding of how life works for us and where it does not. We are better able to remove some of the chaos that we are unknowingly creating and replace it with a happier and peaceful life. The "random" drama and chaos will gently peel away, and you will find that you are in flow with life, rather than fighting against it. If you are one of those people who think you are the healthy one out there in the world, ask yourself these questions. "Who do I become when I cannot have my own way? How am I when I am angry? Do I feel comfortable looking into someone's eyes and telling them how much I love them? Can I be vulnerable with friends? What am I afraid of? Is work the only place I can relax and feel great? When I am worried, how do I communicate? Am I destructive to myself or others? Can I easily take responsibility? When I am criticized, how do I react? Am I able to clearly state how I am feeling in any challenging situation?"

Your first step is to journal and get in touch with how you feel and how you felt. The following is a list of feelings to help in your journaling. Be careful to not go into the victim consciousness, meaning that someone is right or wrong, but rather just the place of observation. Act like you are watching a film, the story of your life. If you go into the blame game, that will become the primary story, and you will feel the hurt and poison over and over again. You cannot punish the past; it becomes an unfulfilled desire to want to punish someone who hurt you. The way to heal is to let go of revenge-seeking, and to focus on yourself and how you feel/felt. Instead, have compassion for yourself and others and see yourself as the child when this happened. Know that it was not your fault. Feel love for the child that you were when it happened. When you lovingly accept it, you can better go through the pain it caused.

Some of your feelings you feel when you start investigating your past might feel strange to those of you who have not looked inward for quite some time. They might all feel the same lumped into some coagulated hot mess of gunk. It could take some time to differentiate and identify how you feel, be gentle, and patient with yourself. They are just feelings. If you are afraid, journal about the fear.

11

Your life is worth your own investigation merely because of the fact that you were born. It is your birthright to gain spiritual awareness and insight into your unique soul and its purpose. Only you can help yourself. Now is the opportunity to meet the person you have been running from. Find a willingness you never thought you had. Start your journal and write for at least 15 minutes every day.

CATEGORY OF FEELINGS

JOY AND CONTENTMENT:

Affectionate	Amazed	Amused
Astonished	Calm	Confident
Content	Curious	Delighted
Determined	Eager	Ecstatic
Excited	Friendly	Grateful
Happy	Hopeful	Inspired
Intrigued	Joyful	Loving
Peaceful	Proud	Relaxed
Relieved	Satisfied	Surprised
Thankful	Thrilled	Touched

ANGER AND FRUSTRATION:

Agitated	Angry	Annoyed
Appalled	Disgusted	Frustrated
Furious	Impatient	Indignant
Infuriated	Irritated	Resentful

FEAR AND ANXIETY:

Afraid	Alarmed	Anxious
Apprehensive	Bewildered	Cautious
Concerned	Confused	Disturbed
Dubious	Embarrassed	Jittery
Nervous	Overwhelmed	Panicky
Puzzled	Reluctant	Restless
Scared	Shocked	Terrified
Worried		

SADNESS AND GRIEF:

Bored	Depressed	Disappointed
Discouraged	Dismayed	Exhausted
Helpless	Hopeless	Hurt
Lonely	Melancholic	Sad
Tired	Troubled	

JOURNAL

HOW WAS I WOUNDED OR HURT AS A CHILD? WHAT HAPPENED?

HOW DID THAT (EACH INCIDENT) MAKE ME FEEL?

WHAT EVENT FROM MY CHILDHOOD IS MOST DIFFICULT TO LET GO OF?

WHAT FEELINGS DO I HOLD ON TO BECAUSE OF IT?

HOW DO I FEEL WHEN I WAKE UP?

HOW DO I FEEL WHEN I SEE OTHERS SUCCEED AND BE HAPPY?

WHAT FEELINGS DO I TRY TO AVOID OR DENY?

FEELINGS CONFUSE ME, BECAUSE....

CHAPTER TWO

Obstacles On Your Journey

In any good story or film, the hero has many obstacles along his journey of transformation. It is never a straight line, and it is never easy. These are called plot twists, and it is what makes the story interesting. We especially love it if the obstacles are unpredictable and outlandish. We are pulled into the story and even try to solve the problems in order to help our hero. If only we had the same outlook about the obstacles in our lives!

We will always have outside influences and obstacles that we have no control over in our lives. Things happen: family members get sick, we have to move, our company closes its doors, our car breaks down, or we see our ex- is happily married! Life can suck sometimes. But it is your reaction to these events that will tell a lot about you. We see some people glide through life no matter what is thrown at them. You might wonder, how can I be more like them?

What is going to snag you are your inner obstacles, also known as your limiting beliefs. We invite you to walk the dark halls of your mind to find out what is holding you back, what ideas and beliefs are limiting you from being all that you could be. You might need to throw several lifelong conceptions out the window, and it won't be easy. But we can guarantee it will be worth it.

Every time you endured a wound, it caused a perversion in your beliefs, emotions, and attitudes. For example, if you were sexually abused, you might have a theory that men or women cannot be trusted. Or you might believe that love hurts and is confusing; or that this is how you get attention from someone, you have sex with them. You might think that you are bad because this happened; you are not a good person. You might be left with the belief that you don't deserve to have someone treat you well. A fixed mindset could be, I cannot say no to sex, people just hurt me, I hate men or women, and/or life feels so unfair and burdensome. The list could go on and on and on.

Limiting beliefs create a breakdown in our life experience. They were set up by our observations when we were unable to ascertain the entire reality of the situation. We are dragging around our reality of the world, and it is not working for us! We don't even realize that just because we believe something, does not make it true. Just because it is in your mind, does not make it accurate. In fact, if it is limiting, it is NOT true, and it can be changed. You have the power to change it.

BELIEFS CREATE YOUR THOUGHTS.........CREATE YOUR FEELINGS..........CREATE YOUR ACTIONS........CREATE YOUR RESULTS.

BELIEFS CREATE YOUR RESULTS

I was bullied all my life. I just wanted someone to come and rescue me, to make it go away. I felt like I had no power to make it stop. I did not know what to do. I thought there was something wrong with me, that I was not as good as the other kids. I withdrew and hated school, and my grades suffered. I did not have many friends. I started believing that I could not do anything well. I just wanted to die, to make it all go away.

All of your wounds cause you to believe something about yourself that is not true. Or they could cause you to think something about society that is not true, something about the family structure, relationships, money, men, women, religion, God, and any other category in the world. Some of your best ideas keep you locked up and in bondage to yourself!

Most people can drastically change the quality of their lives by just changing 5-10 of their limiting beliefs. What is a belief? It is an opinion, a thought, an interpretation, a representation about something or someone. Does that definition sound like something that is set in stone? Our beliefs actually change many times over our lifetime. We can also become very stubborn over our ideas, insisting they are the correct beliefs and others are wrong. Beliefs cannot be proven, only defended.

Living by limiting beliefs is like showing up to the play in the wrong costume. Life does not flow well; your story does not match the reality of what is happening. You could be in an identity crisis, trying to live by what others want and trying to fit in too much. But your life will actually become more vibrant and more profound the more you get to know yourself and as you change what does not work. Your fears will drop away, and you will build the courage to live life as the real you and not what others want. Your outer world and inner world will line up, and you will begin to flow through life instead of resisting it.

Dr. Masaru Emoto spent his life investigating water and the effects of prayer and positive thoughts and intention on it. This is important because we are made up of approximately 76% water. His first experiment was done on some very polluted water in a lake. He took samples and then put them under a high-powered microscope. Then he took several monks to the water, and they prayed over the water for several minutes. He again took samples and photographed the results under his high-powered microscope.

The results were astonishing. The differences in the water molecules were like night and day. The water crystals that were prayed over and sent positive thoughts were beautiful clear crystalline geometric structures. The polluted water had brown, disfigured shapes that were not beautiful to look at. To see his results and to read more about him, visit his website at www.masaru-emoto.net.

He continued to experiment by saying negative words into the water and taking microscopic photographs of each negative word water crystal or phrase, like, 'I hate you.' There was a signature look for each negative thought or word. Conversely, each positive phrase or a word like, 'I love you' looked very different. His work is controversial because it involves what we call the unseen realm or consciousness. But his simple experiment with rice in water is easy for everyone to duplicate at home. If you have three containers of rice and a little bit of water, simply put a lid on each of them and label them, I love you, I hate you, and nothing on the third jar.

Every day speak to jar #1 and #2, saying what the label states, I love you or I hate you. The third jar you will ignore and give no attention. Surprisingly, the jars are very different at the end of a month. Jar #1, I love you, will have the least amount of mold if any. Jar #2 will show some mold inside. But the most mold will grow in the jar that you gave no attention to, you ignored it! He concluded that being ignored is much worse than being given negative attention and criticism.

Most of us have a good amount of negative self-talk every day. What is this doing to our bodies and attitudes? How is this affecting our passion for life or our enthusiasm for trying new things if we symbolically throw cold water on them before trying? Our words and thoughts matter a lot, even if you don't believe in the direct correlation that Dr. Emoto hypothesized. We have experienced that we can be wholly disheartened when a person criticizes our efforts rather than encourages us to keep going.

What about our longstanding beliefs about relationships, the world, men, women, money, and religion? Have you ever thought to really investigate what they are and how they might be affecting your life? What if you have a belief that, 'I am better than everyone else.' This might influence your ability for interconnectedness with others. This could make someone a tyrant, bully, or dictator. If there is no room for anyone else in your life, what quality of relationships will you have? Is this a belief that is working for you? Probably not.

I always wanted to find the next fix, find anything to ease my pain. It might be alcohol; it might be angel dust. Anything to make me feel happy for a few minutes or hours. I was selfish and self-seeking, never having compassion for my fellow man. My thought was always, "What's in it for me?" When I finally got sober and started working on my inner demons, my life transformed. Now, I live by the motto: If you recognize every man as a Holy man, then you have a happy day.

There are always indicators and evidence within your personal relationships, such as:

- Are you argumentative?
- Do you have low self-esteem?
- Is your life unmanageable?
- Do you burn bridges?
- Are you angry with people?
- Are you resentful?
- Are you irritable?
- Do you have low coping skills?
- Do you have a lot of jealousy?
- Do you need always to get your way?

If so, who is running the show? If your old wounds and limiting beliefs are, you are not in control of your emotional nature. If you have a big reaction to many things and people, you are not in control of your emotional life. If you have emotional outbursts or are hugely offended every day or week, you have some real inner work to do on yourself.

For example, the father that always picked up the younger brother affected the big sister. She felt like her father liked her brother more than her. She could then develop limiting beliefs based on this wound such as, I am not lovable, I am not good enough, boys are better than girls, or, I have to be loud to get his attention. This limiting belief affects her behavior. She might become outrageous in her tone and dress, always wanting to attract some boy's attention. This behavior could lead to unfavorable consequences, even putting her in dangerous situations with the opposite sex. If she reacted the opposite way, always wanting to hide and be invisible, she would limit the quality of her relationships with others too.

When I was born, my mother contracted tuberculosis, and I was therefore isolated from her. I never had the chance to connect and bond with her. In the nursery, I used to gasp for air and just look up at the ceiling. When my dad visited, I would just turn away. When my mom finally came home weeks later, I did not even like for her to pick me up or touch me. Even when I got older, I felt like she was not my mom, and I did not belong in that family. I kept waiting for someone to come and rescue me. I was never encouraged at home. At school, they always picked someone else. I gave up trying and became rebellious. The system was not for me, did not work for me. I just wanted to get by, I seemed to be out of rhythm with everyone else. I felt out of touch with me, who was I? Mostly I felt ashamed and inadequate. Maybe I belonged on another planet because this place just felt too cruel.

Some examples of limiting beliefs around relationships are:

1. Men need to control women

2. Men are the providers and protectors of women

3. Women should stay home and cook, clean, or take care of kids and never be the primary provider for the family

4. Affection is best initiated from men

5. Women cannot be trusted

6. Same-sex love relationships are just wrong
7. The way to show affection is to criticize
8. Love hurts
9. Being truthful is not right in a close relationship
10. There is always a power play between people living together

These are limiting because they limit the way you show love, restrict your ability to show your love, and ultimately limit you in fully expressing yourself as a healthy human being. These limiting beliefs cost you – they cost you in making powerful choices for yourself. If you limit what you give, you will limit what you receive. Limiting beliefs keep us from being and living who we truly are, from not being able to live to our fullest potential.

When an actor lands a new job, one of the first things they will do is start journaling about their new character. There is only so much the writer can put in a two-hour script, so much of the back story is left out. They want to know who the character really is. What happened to them when they were four years old, for example. What do they believe in? Why? What are they afraid of? What do they really want? This is real work to investigate and examine a character to make them multi-dimensional. But this is the only way to play an authentic and consistent role in a film. The actors that put in this extra work are the ones earning the academy awards.

Just like those actors, the quality of your life will start showing up the more authentic you become, the more you peel away old limiting beliefs and attitudes that do not serve you. The artist Prince was unfortunately teased and maybe even bullied in school. But unlike most people, because of that, he chose to become more outlandish in his appearance while he was performing. This was a choice that worked for him; it was one of the things that set him apart from other performers. So, from our wounds, we can make choices that do work for us, that serve us in becoming all we can be.

One of the best examples of this is the true story of a new kid in a Canadian school who was bullied and teased. Instead of being a victim, Josh decided to start opening and holding doors for everyone instead of reacting badly to what life was throwing in his path. Slowly, but surely, the kids began seeing Josh and even saying good morning back to him. Even though Josh felt like hiding, he courageously faced the bullying in a heart-centered way and turned the school around. Everyone at the school became kinder and more compassionate to others. He is now widely and affectionately known as, The Doorman. Josh turned the obstacles into an opportunity.

Most of us have toxic members in our families. We have an idea that other families look happy, get along, and have excellent communication. We try and live up to what our family wants us to. We adapt ourselves to fit in or to hide secrets. We stuff the pain and the memories because we really want that ideal, beautiful family. But there is a price to pay for hiding, and for trying to be something that we aren't, for not being authentic human beings. It creates a stagnation to our growth and development.

I stood outside the room in the hospital and listened to someone speak terrible things about me. I put all this work into myself, and I let someone else's words make me feel awful. Then I realized that this is the same pattern that has been happening for many years.

I was in this program for many months, and on my last weekend pass, I came home to show my mom. When I got to the front door, my mom said, "I don't feel like being bothered right now. She had not seen me in 6 months. I just stood there; I thought she was playing around. Then I started crying, set down my book and materials, and went out and got loaded. I threw it all away.

Most of us would love to win the lottery. We have fantasies of how we would spend all that money. But most of us do not buy lottery tickets. Why? Because we don't believe that we will win. We act on the belief, not the desire. We can see this with our passion for a better job, a more fulfilling relationship, a higher education degree, or to travel around the world. It is human nature to act from our belief or expectation of what will happen rather than from our desires.

This is how we become stuck and feel like we cannot change anything in our lives. We become frustrated because we want something better but can't seem to achieve it. Many people do not even fully understand why they are not acting on their desires. They do not see that their choices are creating an outcome that is not wanted. The options are not coming from what they want, but they are coming from what they believe is possible. They are left with a feeling that they cannot get what they really want.

How can you change your limiting beliefs? The first step is to become aware of them. You cannot change anything that you are not aware of. Makes sense, right? Many times, just bringing an old belief into your consciousness is enough to transform it. It will seem magical to you when it happens. Other times you will need to put more work into changing a limiting belief into one you desire, into one that works toward creating the life you want.

Jung said, "We cannot change anything until we accept it. Condemnation does not liberate, it oppresses."

A tool called Emotional Freedom Technique (EFT) can help you with the stubborn beliefs that don't seem to change. This was created by Gary Craig around 1990 and is related to Acupuncture and Acupressure in that you can self-administer tapping to some points in your body to release negative trapped emotions. This might seem impossible to you or even ridiculous, but there is another type of therapy that is used by psychologists worldwide.

EFT is similar to Eye Movement Desensitization and Reprocessing (EMDR) in that both techniques can release negative thoughts and emotions.

EMDR was discovered by Francine Shapiro, Ph.D., who realized the therapeutic effects quite by accident. It has been practiced in the U.S. and around the world for the past 25 years. Dr. Shapiro found that emotional and behavioral symptoms resulting from traumatic experiences can be resolved naturally when a person allows him/ herself to recall various elements of memory while engaging in bilateral stimulation such as lateral eye movements. While you are focusing on an object like a pencil and moving your eyes from left to right while recalling the traumatic event, it can lead to safe processing of memories, in that the negative thoughts and emotions disappear.

EFT is much easier to self-administer and can be used for unwanted negative emotions, thoughts, or situations in your past. First, imagine a past event that was painful for you. Rate it on a scale of 1-10, with 10 being the most painful. The following is just an example, it will be more powerful when you insert your own thoughts and feelings into your release because it will be more personal to you.

SAMPLE:

(Tap on karate point of your hand)
Say three times: Even though I have all these negative thoughts and emotions, I completely love and accept myself.

(Tap on your Eyebrow 7 times)
Say: All these negative thoughts.

(Tap on the side of Eye 7 times)
Say: All these negative emotions.

(Tap under Eye 7 times)
Say: So hard to stop them once they start.

(Tap under Nose 7 times)
Say: There's nothing wrong with me.

(Tap on Chin 7 times)
Say: It's how my brain is wired.

(Tap on Clavicle 7 times)
Say: But I can start to change it.

(Tap on top of Head 7 times)
Say: I can tell my brain that it's OK to relax.

Make sure you are breathing!
Go through all points again saying,
I am safe now.
It's safe to feel positive.
The universe supports me.
I am strong.
I am loved.
I feel wonderful.
I am always supported and safe.
BREATHE!

Now rate the past experience again on a scale of 1-10. Hopefully, the number has diminished, if not, do another round of tapping and measure it again. It might take several rounds of tapping, but usually, people feel a release after the first round. Observe if your mind interferes with the real experience and tap on your resistance!

You can extensively read about both alternative therapies online, and there will be some positive and some negative information for both. Ultimately you are the best judge, however; so simply try it and see if you can get some relief. If you walk away with a more significant sense of peace while you remember or recount the same issue you tapped on, that is a success! It is working.

Remember that all traumas also leave you with a limited belief. If you were abused by men, you might believe that all men are unsafe. Many of your limiting beliefs are in your subconscious brain, so journaling on topics such as Men are......Women are..... Try and use a stream of consciousness, just write without editing or rewriting to see what comes out. You might be surprised at some of the gems that just pop out when your analytical mind is not in control.

The limiting beliefs will be the next ones to target in your tapping sessions. Keep track in your journal regarding the limiting belief and the level of discomfort. You may go back at any time and reassess the opinion. Is it still a minor discomfort, or do you need to tap some more? Document what beliefs you desire to replace the limiting belief with. Perhaps an empowering thought such as: I know which men are safe at all times.

JOURNAL

MEN ARE:

WOMEN ARE:

MONEY IS:

_____
_____
_____
_____
_____
_____
_____
_____
_____
_____
_____
_____
_____
_____
_____
_____
_____
_____
_____
_____
_____
_____
_____
_____
_____
_____
_____
_____
_____

LIFE IS:

MY MOTHER WAS/IS:

MY FATHER WAS/IS:

I BELIEVE:

LOVE IS:

CHAPTER THREE

Are You A Bad Actor In A 'B' Movie On A Bad Day?

A quote by Dr. Carl Jung, a noted psychologist who was mentored by Dr. Sigmund Freud is appropriate for this chapter. ***"One does not become enlightened by imagining figures of light but by making the darkness conscious."***

It is even more interesting when we dissect what is meant by this simple statement and find out how powerful and profound it is. Even if your goal is not to become enlightened, but to merely become the best you possible, it cannot be done without embracing your darkness. No one will get there by doing positive affirmations or meditating on love and light. It is not accomplished by ignoring your wounds and the part of your past you are ashamed of. Your blissful prayers or chanting will not bring you to the place of enlightenment either. But looking at your dark side will.

What is your darkness? It is your ego. It is your dark nature that wants to be right all the time. It is the self-serving aspect of yourself that is not heart-centered. It is the side of you that is not honest, that manipulates to get your own way, that denies you are anything but kind and giving. It is your selfish side. It is the part of you that blames others. It is the part of you that is service to self and not in service to others. And we all have this dark side; no one is above it or better than anyone else. It's just that some people are better at hiding it than others.

When we operate under the belief or distortion that we are really the "good person" and the problem is outside of ourselves, we become fragmented. We cannot integrate our dark side into our whole being if we deny it. If we continuously push our darkness away, we are denying a big part of ourselves. Our lives become compartmentalized if we are fragmented. We will act one way at work, show another side of ourselves to one group of friends, and even hide parts of ourselves to yet another group. Our personality will continuously try and build smoke screens to protect the part of ourselves we deny and hide.

If you are operating out of your ego, your personality, your wounds, and your limiting beliefs, you will never achieve the goals you so desire. Your life will continue to be full of chaos and disappointments if you do not embrace your dark side. If you do not go through all of your pain and resentments to reach the other side, your life cannot move forward in a healthy way. Your claim to fame will be that you will only be a bad actor in a B movie on a bad day. Dr. Jung asserted, *"There is no coming to consciousness without pain."*

It takes honesty and courage to face ourselves on a deep level, and so this is one of the most critical steps. Denial is the trickster in your story. It will try and protect the personality at all costs, and it will trick you. You have lied to yourself so many times that the lies seem like the truth. You have no idea you are in denial, and you cannot see it, but others can. And your life is mirroring this fact back to you in the way of disconnection from others, conflicts with many people, a feeling of emptiness, depression, or a lack of interest in anything and anyone.

I would get two quarts of beer every night in part to be ready for the next day. I drank one at night and saved one for the following day because I had alienated myself from all of my so-called friends who did not share their beer with me. I was angry and felt like a victim of my circumstances and blamed everyone else. Now I was 49 years old, and I was sitting in the parking lot alone and homeless. I said to myself, "Is this it?" I used to go into the McDonald's to wash my face every day, but this time I heard a voice say, 'You know, you have been washing your face in McDonald's for some time now. You don't want to get kicked out of there... of all places. I really looked into the mirror and left to wash my face in cold water on the beach. Everything got really quiet...no birds, no airplanes, no thoughts in my head, an eerie silence and stillness. I was surprised more than anything. I was just stripped naked... no facades...saw all the characters I was putting on for others... saw the truth about all I was trying to be. I was a fraud. I felt so hurt, so much shame and so powerless to do anything about my situation. I was not looking for God. I did not feel I had a right to call on God. But I feel he was with me that day, to help me see the truth of my situation and who was really to

41

blame. Me. I had to first give up my need to know and control everything. I had to start at a point zero in order to recover.

You must be willing to be vulnerable with yourself and others to find the truth. This type of honesty must move through your fear and shame. This step is the most difficult to master, and it is the most important. Your mind can tell you there are many grey areas in situations and your thoughts and emotions play with that, but ultimately, you are either being honest, or you are not. The negative patterns can be broken with the principle of honesty. When you switch the observation point, you are adding fuel for integrating all parts of yourself into an authentic life.

According to Jung, our psyche does react badly when we act as if some parts of us aren't really ours. If we continually search for external reasons why we behave the way we do or we want to hide the parts we dislike from the world, including from ourselves, we end up with a personality that is split, or, "*unwhole.*" In other words, we are fragmented and it would be impossible to be authentic.

There are many indicators of not living authentically. If you want to please everyone and anybody, it is an indicator of being fragmented. You might try to be all things to all people, even going against things you believe in. Perhaps you find it difficult to say no. Are you uncomfortable sticking up for yourself? Do you feel like a doormat? Do people take advantage of your kindness? If so, you will probably feel shame and anger for not being able to stick up for yourself, for going along with something that you don't believe in, or feeling manipulated and used by others. You went along with the crowd, doing things that you would never do alone, and now you have to live with yourself. You bury it, further alienating yourself from your authentic self. These become ghosts from your past, continually making you feel uncomfortable, contributing to the dark hole inside.

None of this is wrong or right, bad or good. It is just a place where the individual finds himself in his life, codes of conduct, or the way he believes. These are just some of the conditions we have to visit in order to integrate ourselves so that we can become more authentic. Some of the conditions run our lives, and we deny them, but if we are left feeling unsatisfied and unhappy, there is a reason for it.

What does it look like when you become a B actor in a B movie on a bad day?

You could be telling yourself that you can give up drinking anytime that you want. You don't have a problem, right? You just don't want to quit. You like to drink. But when you have tried in the past, your thoughts become obsessive about drinking. You are miserable living with yourself, and the desire to drink builds and builds until you cave in. So you drink, and now you tell yourself that you only drink a little bit, others have the drinking problem, you are just fine.

Or maybe you tell yourself that you don't have a problem, you just like to hang out and have fun with your friends. Perhaps your story is that nothing is going to happen to you if you only do a little bit of drinking or drugs on the weekend. No one will find out. If you are not thinking about realistic consequences, you are in denial. If you are not investigating how it affects all of your relationships, you are lying to yourself.

You could be saying that you know yourself and you don't have a problem. But if you don't know your limitations and weaknesses, they will capture you in your weak moments and take over your life. You must know your dark side as well as your light side. What are your trigger points with your thoughts and emotions? How reactive are you with people? Even if you try to ignore it, your wounds are emitting messages that are making you uncomfortable and uneasy.

The evidence will come up that you have tricked yourself again. The evidence is stronger than the words that you know yourself. If you don't want to do a thorough investigation because it feels terrible and overwhelming or shameful, then you are still wounded. You do not know yourself if you have not admitted the worst part of yourself. This will keep you in bondage, and only you can set yourself free by facing that part of yourself.

You must first recognize your dishonesty with an attitude of acceptance so that honesty can guide the mind. Honesty is consistent. There are no gray areas. You are either telling the truth, or you are not. The mind can come up with a lot of answers, but only one is correct. Your mind can tell you there are many gray areas in situations and the thoughts and emotions play with that, but ultimately, you are either being honest, or you are not. Alternative facts and hyperbole are lies. If you believe otherwise, your mind is playing tricks on you.

Why do you lie? You lie to control and manipulate others. You lie to hide from yourself. Lying can become a bad habit that you have no control over. You can become obsessive in trying to conceal your dark self from others. But you can never change any pattern without first becoming aware of it; without first being honest about it. This takes rigorous honesty without compromise.

> *I used to do this verbal 'squidding' where I would squirt out a lot of bullshit so that people could not find me. Like when an octopus squirts out ink to hide from his predators. I was metaphorically putting up a smoke screen so that I would not be judged or ridiculed. It felt safe for me. But the moment I knew it was OK to say, "I don't know," was the moment when real spiritual growth started for me. I did not need a joke or a lie anymore, just the truth. I had a taste of real freedom, and it felt great.*

What does it mean to be a B actor in a B movie on a bad day? It is when you are living out of your habits, unconscious to why you behave a certain way. It is when you are living from your wounds and traumas and are unaware they are running the show. It is when you have become so fragmented within yourself, that there is no authenticity anymore. It is when your mind tricks you over and over again with distorted thinking, rationalizations, and justifications.

Justification and rationalization without investigation keep you in a slump and makes you go bump in your life. It will affect your self-esteem. You could wake up irritable, in a slump. When you start knowing yourself, confidence returns. When you start taking responsibility for yourself, you stop having an excuse for everything. Only then can you start having a personal relationship with yourself as your habits dissolve away.

If you deny your bad habits, that doesn't make them go away. That is how a child might think; it is magical thinking. A habit takes away your options. It will plan your day for you. It will come knocking on your door, and before you know it, you have gone down a path you swore that you wouldn't. It will take away any possible choice you might hope for. You are trapped, and you don't know you are trapped. No one needs to live in shame for their past mistakes, and your future can be better. Living from a place of freedom is having many options available for you.

The movie, Shaka Zula, shows how best to catch a monkey. They place shiny objects in a gourd with a small opening, and when the monkey tries to grab them, he refuses to release them, thereby allowing his hand to dislodge from the gourd easily. He could easily escape the jar, but he is trapped. The monkey mind is always trying to grab shiny objects, and it too becomes a trap. Greed traps you; selfish desires trap you. When you have nothing, you have everything. Let go of everything that brings inconsistency into your character. Then you can stand up and appreciate your life. Your life belongs to you, and it is sacred. Guilt and shame cannot come to your house selling you products like you are not good enough.

How can your mind trick you? Let's say you made an agreement with someone to take a certain percentage for your commission. You are in charge of paying them the overage you received. When the time comes to pay, you see all the money in your account, and you don't really want to part with it. Your mind comes up with all sorts of ideas why you don't have to. You start to feel like you deserve a more significant percentage, and you justify it in your mind. So, you just ignore the phone calls from the person you owe money to and make them the bad guy. You start to say nasty things about that person, who is merely wishing you will make good on your agreement.

Or you borrow money from a friend, and when the time comes to pay it back, your mind takes over, and you start to justify why you don't have to pay it back. You see their thick wallet that has bills stuffed into it. You think that person has a lot more money than you, so why should you give them more money when you don't have any? They don't even need it you say to yourself. They are just greedy because they want your little bit of money. And you believe these lies!

Even if no one believes you, the truth is still the truth. And even if everyone believes you, a lie is still a lie. The real question is, what was your contract or agreement? Did you honor it?

You might be in an abusive relationship and continually tell yourself that things are not that bad, or that he/she had a bad day at work, they did not mean to do whatever they did. You continually make excuses for bad behavior. You are never looking at the truth of the situation, that this might not be a healthy place for you. That environment is slowly killing you by eating away at your self-esteem and independence, and you are lying to yourself. But others can watch how your potential diminishes, and you become a puppet for the other person. Staying in a toxic environment like this prohibits you from becoming your authentic self, experiencing the depths of all that you could be.

Your Dr. reported that your potassium levels are low and suggested you eat bananas. You are really overweight, prediabetic, and know you need to lose some weight. You get a banana cream pie and tell yourself, 'This is the same thing as eating bananas, right?" You try your best to make yourself feel good about your decision, but underneath the guilt and shame is creeping up on you.

You need to exercise more but really don't like it. You try to set up a reward for yourself like a new pair of running shoes after 7 days. You are motivated for one day. But then your mind starts playing games with you, and you tell yourself you need new shoes to run well and not hurt yourself. So, you go and buy yourself the reward you were supposed to be waiting for. But when tomorrow comes there is no workout because you already got your new shoes. And you justify all of these rationalizations until guilt and shame come knocking on your door.

The principle of honesty is not present when you are justifying or rationalizing whatever it is that you want to do. When there is not that thorough investigation you are in danger of becoming a NIKE commercial; your mind will say to you, 'Just do it,' without looking at the consequences. Now your habit is running your life, whatever that habit might be. It becomes a compulsion, an obsession. Addiction is obsessive, compulsive behavior disorder. It takes away your freedom to choose; you are enslaved by the habit.

You just got out of a rehab center, and it is your birthday. You want to feel good, and you tell yourself you deserve just to celebrate your birthday. So, you smoke a joint, drink a beer, and to keep from hearing the truth about it, you pretend this one time does not count. It does not matter because you have not relapsed in your mind. You are only celebrating your birthday. You forget what drove you into rehab in the first place, the unmanageability of your life.

You are not good with money. You made a commitment to do better and pay off your credit cards. But this new sweater catches your eye. You don't need it, but you really, really want it. You tell yourself you deserve this reward for all the hard work this month. Your mind goes into overdrive about why it is OK to buy this one sweater, and you promise you will start saving next month. Procrastination becomes a haven for more and more lies that you tell yourself. It is like fertile ground for rationalizations, justifications, lies, and smoke screens to the truth.

A principle like honesty is alive; it cannot turn upon itself. If you tell yourself that you are an honest person and you start to feel uncomfortable, it's like deep down, you know better. The only thing that will make you start living honestly is when dishonesty is pointed out. You must first make the commitment to live by this principle. You will then begin to live that honesty, and you start to make decisions that don't compromise you or put you in a position to lie.

Sometimes a person is not setting out to lie. He is trying to find his comfort. He has to sell the story. That story could be something that they really want to believe. Like they are really religious because they go to church on Sunday. They are a good person. But during the rest of the week, they live these ungodly lives, cheating, lying, manipulating. They could say, "I am only human," if caught. This is another way of lying to yourself. The first recipient of the lie is the individual himself.

Having your nose in your cell phone has become an epidemic today. Millions of people are addicted and don't realize it because they have never questioned it. The device is set up to be addicting, much like slot machines in Vegas. Can you leave it at home if you go out to eat with friends? Can you go on a vacation and read a book instead of checking your email or text messages? If the device is controlling you, then it has become a habit, and you are not in control of it.

Most people don't think they lie to themselves. They say, "I am an honest person." The thought of being dishonest or a liar is not a place they want to be. What are you lying to yourself about?

What is the worst possible thing that could happen if you decided to be honest? Maybe you think that life would be boring or that you would not have any fun if you had to tell the truth.

Some lies are so devastating that the change could be forced, but there is a prolonged agony because you usually have to keep feeding the lies with more and more lies. It can build up fast. You can lie yourself into oblivion, and it becomes a way of life. The elaborate story does not allow the individual to see the story of where they came from. All great lies come with a good story.

Let's say you deal drugs, but you don't think about who you are hurting. You only focus on making such good money, but you are in a lifestyle that becomes dangerous. You tell yourself that you cannot go to work for minimum wage, you deserve fast, good money. But your ambitions and dreams are squashed, and this drug environment becomes a way of life. Then you start living your selfishness, and you are incredibly self-centered. Everything revolves around you. You have to surround yourself with people you trust, but that becomes impossible.

Some drug dealers say they sell drugs because they are helping people because that is what the person wants. You are providing a service to people, just like the Robin Hood effect. Many drug dealers say they are no different than the governments who have been caught in corruption and oppression of the people. The system is against them, so why not be as corrupt as the CIA, police, government, you name it. We all lie to ourselves. It becomes a coping mechanism to help us through. We see it as a means to an end.

If you have a gambling problem, it is too easy to hide from your loved ones. There is no alcohol on your breath, no change in your behavior like with drugs, only the dwindling bank account when it is over or the bookies calling for their money. But you told yourself that you could win this time, you felt it in your bones! That you needed to win all the money back that you lost. The problem is that if you were lucky enough to win, your story would then change. Now you are on a winning streak and gamble again to get ahead.

The real indicator or evidence of how much you lie to yourself is within your relationships. What is the quality of your intimate relationships? All relationships with yourself and others need to embody the Five C's to be healthy:

Commitment, Communication, Cooperation, Consideration, and Compromise.

Commitment begins with the agreement you have with yourself and/or another person. Your commitment might be that you will honor abstinence no matter what condition you might find yourself in. You will never try and make yourself feel better with an outside substance. That substance could be sugar, alcohol, or drugs, sex, or gambling. Your commitment to another person might be that you are committed to honesty and faithfulness. What is your agreement with your loved one?

What quality of communication do you have with yourself and your loved one? What is your thought like that affects your emotions? Are you being clear and kind? Are you truly listening? Are you just trying to be right? Are you being honest with yourself about what you are feeling and why? Are you able to be vulnerable? Can you accept what someone is saying and not let your old patterns rob you of spiritually growing? Can you keep that honest appraisal so that you don't fall into any old pattern that tends to distort who you are or what the relationship is about? Are you too critical? Are you controlling? Are you blaming someone else for your emotions?

I was in a relationship for 7 years and was frustrated by our communication much of the time. My partner could only talk about work, and he was a workaholic. There was never any vulnerability or talk about our plans as a couple. He never shared how much money he made. He never shared how he felt about us. We never talked about moving in together, he just planted himself at my house. I kept telling myself it will get better. It did not, and now that I look back, I have to ask, better than what? I was just lying to myself.

Cooperation is working well with others to achieve something. It allows you to mirror the best qualities of yourself to share with another. Or do you need to get your way most of the time? Is it hard for the fluidity of cooperation to be present? Would you really instead desire that everyone just listened to you and did what you said? You tell yourself that would be so much easier, but the reality is that it would not be better. Everyone likes and needs to be heard and to feel valued. Only cooperation can achieve this.

Consideration is careful thought, typically over a period of time. This is impossible if you are a narcissist or selfish, as you only see things through your eyes. This takes an ability to put yourself into the other person's shoes and to see where they are coming from. To be able to put your needs in second place for a little while, until you can see both sides of an issue. You might also need to use compromise to help come to another solution you both can live with.

My partner wanted me to stop singing a song and playing my guitar because I had been repeating lyrics over and over for 45 minutes. She needed a break. This time I was able to observe my old pattern trying to take over - my mom and siblings were criticizing me and putting me down when I tried to learn a musical instrument. Back then, I felt I was not good enough. But with an honest appraisal, I realized that it had nothing to do with my old pattern. It had to do with sharing space and being considerate of her. I was able to share all of this with her, and of course, I stopped playing and singing.

Compromise is when you can settle a dispute by mutual concession. That means that each side makes concessions. We all want our own way; it is human nature. It is also impossible to achieve unless you are a dictator. If there is no compromise, you are being bullied or are bullying others. You become impossible to be around if you are bullying others, and there is no real intimacy because people cannot be honest with you. Why wouldn't you want to compromise with your loved one if you truly love and respect that person?

Do you want to just be a B actor in a B movie on a bad day? Or would you rather be the actor getting an academy award? If you are in that category of the best of the best, you need to be authentic within yourself. Your character must be consistent, real, and honest. This honesty can set you free so that some salesman does not come knocking on your door trying to sell you something you don't want.

You must do an honest assessment of any addictions or habits you have. If the practice is controlling you, it has become addictive. If you cannot stop a bad habit without having obsessive thoughts and a compulsion to continue it, it is an addiction. If you find yourself rationalizing or justifying a bad habit, it is an addiction. You will not be able to change anything that you are not aware of. Honesty is the first step.

Do you smoke? Are you thinking about having one before breakfast even ends? That is a habit... which takes away choice. Sure, you can choose to stop and not have a cigarette for a day or two, but guess what? Pretty soon you will be lighting one up without thinking about it! Let's be real with ourselves. If you have a habit, you are continually thinking about how to get what you want.

Let principles like honesty lead your life instead of your wounds, your limiting beliefs, your stories, your dramas, your chaos, your habits, your feelings, or your personality. You will start to get different results when you let honesty and awareness guide your life. Your transparency will alleviate your selfishness and self-centered behavior. The evidence will be in the waste management area of your life; you will not be creating toxic environments. And you will rise up out of being a B actor in a B movie on a bad day in Bedrock!

JOURNAL

THE SECRET(S) I AM HIDING FROM OTHERS IS/ARE... WHY?

AM I THE SAME PERSON BEHIND CLOSED DOORS AS I AM IN PUBLIC?

AM I THE SAME PERSON WITH ALL OF MY FRIENDS?

IF I COULD WEAR A MASK IN PUBLIC AND DO ANYTHING I WANTED, WHAT KIND OF A PERSON WOULD I BE?

WHAT FEELINGS ARE SCARY TO FEEL?

WHAT HABITS DO I WANT TO BREAK?

IF I COULD CHANGE ONE THING IN MY LIFE, WHAT WOULD IT BE?

CHAPTER FOUR

Get An A - List Director

In Hollywood, you are categorized into lists according to how 'bankable' you are. In other words, how much money do the powers that be think they can make off of your name and talent? There are A-List actors, directors, and writers who have earned their place into the top ranking because of how much their films have grossed. This happens when the studios feel your track record earns you a spot on the elite team of players in your field. There are B-lists, C-lists, and D-lists too. Obviously, the higher your ranking, the more money you will make, and the more power you have on your film project. The Hollywood industry and most other people view you as more successful if you are on that A-list.

So, let's say you have a great script that was written by an unknown writer. You want to get it produced so you will do your very best to get A-list talent attached to your film. Most producers start with top-level directors since they have many more contacts to great actors who want to work with them. It is a major coup to have an A-list director option your script and run with it. They can make magic happen in pre-production, production, and post-production, and can open doors to almost anyone you might need access to.

An A-List director is also able to get the best performance from the actors because they are the best at their craft. Spielberg is an A-list director. Martin Scorsese is also one. These directors can always see the big picture and how each scene will seamlessly fit together to create the best continuity and storyline. They have incredible vision, clarity, and focus. These are the directors who win awards, and most actors want to work with them.

So, who is directing your story? The story of your life? For most of us, it is our analytical mind. This is the part of our brain that can visualize, articulate, conceptualize, and solve problems. While there are a time and place for using our analytical mind, if we continuously live from this place, we will find that we are also full of critical judgments of ourselves and others, fears, and limiting beliefs, because those traits come from our analytical mind too. Coming from this place will only get you limited results and more pain and fear.

Your analytical mind will act as the antagonist in a film. It will always challenge you, it will work against your authentic self. It will create a battlefield of conflict within your mind so that it becomes impossible to find your authentic self. Choosing this director will not win you any academy awards. So how do you get your A-List director? Tap into your inner wisdom, that quiet inner voice that is connected to all that is, God, Source Energy, the Cosmos, the Creator, the Divine, or any word that you are comfortable with. The name is not important, the frequency of that source of energy is.

Some people can hear their inner voice or intuition clearly. They know how to listen deeply within and hear the small voice that is connected to the Divine Source of the universe. This voice will give you the best guidance and always has your best interest at heart. Why? Because it is connected to pure source energy, which is all good, all knowing, and omnipotent. We all have this capability, but when that voice is not acknowledged, used, or cherished, it becomes so subdued and quiet that we cannot hear it anymore. It is still there, but the volume is turned down so low that it becomes useless to us.

Why is the volume so low on the most important voice we need to hear? Maybe you routinely ignore the guidance coming through. Maybe you go so far as to scoff at it or become angry when it tries to guide you. If there is no reward or guidance for how to use this part of yourself, it will just go dormant. It is possible that other people have ridiculed the intuitive information that you shared with them, so you began to turn the volume down for fear of being ridiculed again. And it could be that we were meant to work a little harder for the things that matter; the more effort we exert, the more we value the accomplishment.

The mind and the ego love to take over and has the loudest voice so we can get confused that it is the one we should listen to. The mind can become so clever that it will take us in circles to prove why we are right, and the other person is wrong, keeping us stuck in our distortions and distractions. And we are only left with the consolation prize of being right. Do you really want to hold onto that funky disposition just so you can be right? The need to be right can quickly escalate into an aggressive tendency.

It can make us believe in competition, that only one person can win, that we must fight for everything we want in life. It will lead us to think that resources are limited, and there is not enough for everyone in this world. You might be left with the limiting belief that life is unfair, they are out to get me, and that you are not good enough. All these limiting thoughts come from the analytical mind.

But our intuition or inner knowing is continually trying to communicate with us. Almost everyone has experienced this heightened sense of awareness where the heart is open and connected to a level of wisdom that is far greater than what they usually touch. Most people have experienced levels of clarity and perspective that are powerful. Maybe you have spoken with such wisdom and clarity, that it could have surprised you. Some call it 'The Lightbulb Moment' because the light is being shone on something you had not noticed before. The more that you can tap into this voice and listen and honor it, the stronger it becomes. Meditation is the key to making this happen or any level of quiet introspection. You can start with five minutes a day and work up to what feels comfortable to you.

My partner and I had lost our intimacy, and I kept asking myself, "Is this as good as it gets? Should I be satisfied with this life?" I kept telling myself it was not that bad that I should leave, things could be much worse. And then something much worse happened. We never yelled or fought with each other. But I became so angry one night at his typical bullying behavior toward the desk clerk because he could not understand her English. I blew up and shouted at him. We took it to the room. It escalated with me calling him an asshole and shoving past him to the bathroom He proceeded to shove me against the wall and put me in a neck hold so tight that it cut my lip and bruised my cheek. I was terrified that he would permanently injure my neck, and I froze. But then I heard a voice that said, "Don't worry, your neck is going to be fine. This is just Divine Intervention." I understood everything then. This needed to happen to get my attention and for me to finally leave a relationship that did not work for me. I then started remembering other times that I had heard this guidance, trying to put me on the correct path.

Meditation can be daunting for a lot of people. But are you able to sit for five minutes and not do anything other than to listen? Can you put your phone away and all other distractions and just sit quietly? An open eye meditation is perfectly fine too. Or you can sit with your eyes closed and concentrate on your breathing. Five minutes every day can make a huge difference. You do not need a particular mantra. You do not require specialized training. You will find what works best for you as you try different things before moving into the correct practice for you.

Why should we want to connect to this inner voice? When you are not connected to your inner voice, you are unconscious. You are not making decisions based upon your dreams, deeper desires, or purpose in life, and you are not in touch with your emotions. If you are unconscious, your emotions and hurts, whether perceived or real, are running the show. Your impulses and reactions can take over and cause a lot of chaos and drama. This quickly becomes the road to Hell.

What is the remedy? Take time each day to sit quietly and focus on your breathing and your body. Notice and be present with all the sensations that are going on in your body. If your focus moves outside of yourself, bring it back to your physical body and inner world. The easiest way to do that is to focus on your breathing again. Observe your thoughts and visualize them floating down the river, having no attachment to any of them.

- Ask, "What is my truth?" LISTEN! Do not try and answer it right away as this answer could be coming from your mind only.
- Practice bringing your energy and focus into your heart area. This will make it easier to hear your inner voice.
- Now sense, feel, hear, or see what your truth is; what your answers are.

At first, you might not trust the answers you hear. You might say to yourself, "Well, that cannot be right." Notice how you try and deny that any part of hearing your intuition is not working. And then sit quietly again, and again until you start to really listen and trust the information that is coming through. A sense of peacefulness might settle into your being at being heard for the first time or in a very long time. The truth will always give us a sense of peace and wholeness.

It might be the scariest proposition to stop and sit quietly to listen to your inner voice. You could feel overwhelmed and be bombarded with all the negative self-talk. Instead of giving up, push through the discomfort, and try and find your inner peace and quiet. Acknowledge all that you experience, the good and the bad. Your mind has been controlling your life for so long, it seems normal. You have been run by your emotions for so long thinking they are authentic, but you have not figured out that they are distorted by faulty programming.

The mind is the prison, the prisoner, and the prison guard. It all takes place in the mind; your reality is filtered through your misperceptions, your faulty ideas, and distorted emotions. Your perception is being run by your ideas and emotions. You become entrapped in thoughts like a program being run on your computer. Selfishness and self-centeredness start taking over, and you want to control every aspect of your life and other people's lives too. You become a bad actor.

It would be like showing up to the set and trying to control all aspects of the filming. You want to set the lights in a particular place, to direct the director; and you give the writer notes on the script, and you tell the cinematographer where the camera should go. Chaos would ensue, just as chaos would be rampant in your life if you started acting this way. But, people do it all the time and think nothing of it. They will offer you advice when you don't ask for it. They will tell you how to run your business, how to become more successful, how to make your life better, how to vote, how to eat, how to pray to your God, what to believe, how to exercise, how to talk to your boss, how to dress, and on and on and on until your brain freezes, and you want to run from the room.

If someone has not asked for your assistance, your opinions, or your thoughts, the best advice is to keep them to yourself. Wait for the invitation, or simply ask permission before offering the help you so want to give. You might say, "I have something that might help you. Would you like to hear it?" Then again, sometimes restriction is the best spiritual practice! This is yet another great reason to learn how to listen to your intuition as it can easily guide you through challenging situations. Trust that everyone has all the answers and guidance they need inside of them, and it is their responsibility alone to access this guidance.

Frequently we hear some profound guidance when we are in a state of crisis. When the ego has to let go after we are in a state of surrender, we can hear our intuition more clearly. One way the mind will go quiet is when our defenses are down, the fight is gone, and we will be open to hearing what might be right for us. Although some might see it as a defeated state, it is actually a good defeat. Our ego is crushed, if only for a minute. We are now open to a new way of thinking and being.

Everything used to be about getting the fix. I was a minister with The Church of Living God. One night I caught the #212 bus to visit my ex-wife. I desperately wanted to see her, to be with her. I started smoking crack with her around 2 A.M. The later it gets, the harder it is to buy some crack. Time runs out. She gave me $10.00 to buy a dime rock. I walked three to four miles to the Arco station to get a rock to smoke. I was trying to get back, and the police stopped me. I tried to hide the rock in my glove, but they found it. I knew I was caught. I thought about spending 5 years in the penitentiary. I thought my life means nothing to me. I wanted to die. I thought I have been so unproductive with my life. But then I heard a voice over my own thoughts. It said, 'You will not see one day in the State Penn.' My hope was too fragile, so I did not want to believe that voice. I did not live that kind of life where I listened, but it was enough to stop me from killing myself, to cooperate with the police and to plead my case. I always remembered that voice of inspiration because that was the night that my life changed for the better.

That voice is always with you, always available to you if you can get out of your own way, get out of your ego, of being a know-it-all and surrender to a higher power of wisdom. When that still small voice comes, and we listen and connect to it, we start remembering all the other times that voice came to us in dark moments to comfort and guide us. We know inherently to call this soul searching when we wish to go deeper and find an answer within that is connected to something bigger than our physical self. Everyone has the power to tap into a greater understanding and insight within. It can happen in an instant.

When I would reflect on the moment of my life when everything changed, the moment on the corner when I was arrested for possession, and I realized the small voice was right. I never spent a day in prison after that day. I started remembering other dark moments when that same voice came to me and offered guidance and direction. One time when I was 18 years old, I had just sliced my wrists (thankfully in the wrong way), and the voice was very clear when it said, "You cannot kill yourself because you did not make yourself!" I sobered up and drove myself to the hospital and never tried to do that again. I knew enough to listen to that voice for some reason. That voice has always brought a course change for the better in my life.

When you learn to tap into this wisdom, you start developing a genuine relationship with yourself. You will start looking for that place of peace and understanding, and you will start trusting and believing in yourself. You will stop walking around listening to the Three Stooges in your head! It is beyond the mind chatter, it is a part of your higher self and wisdom. All your relationships will improve as your relationship with yourself improves. It can almost seem magical at times. You will be able to move into contentment and well-being at your discretion. You realize you are in control of your emotions and your behavior and ultimately, your life....if even for a few minutes.

My mind can take me in a thousand different directions, analyzing things, trying to understand everyone and everything. But, ironically, I started getting the best insight when I started meditating. One day an inspired thought came to me, "Why do I always have to be the strong one?" It was so profound I stopped for a moment and remembered thinking that very same thought as a child. I felt like I had to be the parent much of the time, to be the strong one. I realized it became a belief, a self-fulfilling prophecy. I was always the strong one in my relationships, taking care of much more than I should be. I realized I did not have to carry that distorted belief around any longer. I felt a great relief, and my relationships changed for the better.

What are the indicators that you are living from the analytical mind? Your fears are driving your decisions. You are indecisive. You are filled with doubts and insecurities. You have lost hope. When the one person you should trust (yourself), but you don't. You see the world as out to get you, as unsafe. You are filled with jealousies and resentments of people who seem to have figured out this game of life. You become disenfranchised with the social condition in which you find yourself. You want to numb yourself with alcohol, drugs, social media, shopping, food, sex, television, or gambling. You also want to fill up your life with superficial things and material objects. But, your life will become even more miserable as nothing can fill the void except your connection to your authentic self.

It will be more challenging to quiet your mind if you are running on your wounds and limiting beliefs. It will be more difficult if you have let those wounds turn into some sort of addiction. If your mind is preoccupied with obsessive-compulsive thoughts (which is what addiction is), you have little space for the quiet voice. It is challenging to quiet the mind from obsessive thinking; obsessive means you are not in control. Compulsive thoughts and actions are a sign that you are not in control and that your life has become unmanageable.

How do you get rid of obsessive-compulsive thoughts? You heal the wound. You find out what limiting belief you accepted because of this wound. When you realize you have the power to change your mind, you will dare to face your darkest side, things you might not be proud of. You must have the desire to let it all go; all of your old story that is not working for you.

Our emotional disfiguration keeps us from connecting to our authentic selves. However, when we realize that discovering our authentic selves is exciting and rewarding, we will gladly give up the distortions. It is insane to think time and again that our old unhealthy habits will get us different results. When you let go of the false perception you have of yourself, change begins to happen. You will start to enjoy and experience life in a different way.

What is limiting you from being your authentic self? What are some of your fears or doubts? Have you ever made decisions based on fear and realized that the fear only expands? We become a generator of fear, and it takes us further away from our authentic self. When you put a spin on everything, you become a spin master, focusing on all the wrong things. This will keep you in an identity crisis, never realizing the truth about you.

I was having obsessive thoughts throughout the day, 'What if I went back and relapsed?' I kept seeing myself doing it, then I dreamed about it that night. In the morning, I looked at the love of my life. I heard a small voice inside ask me, 'Would he be here if I did that foolish stuff?' The answer was, no. My partner means the world to me. Then I thought about my grandson and everything important to me. When I shifted back into a good place, I realized that that decision would only bring me pain and sorrow. The question brought me back to reality. It brought me to a place of actually having a choice. I had pain, but I did not react to the pain of it like I usually did. I examined myself. That created a bit of freedom for me. I did not go from 0-100 in 3 seconds, back into the bullshit. I realized I had a choice, and I wanted a positive outcome. My brain was on a meltdown, and my spirit came in and showed me another way.

You are a repairman because you are always trying to fix the discomfort. Maybe if I would have done this, you criticize yourself with how to fix it. But you might not be using the right tool. You are always trying to work from the analytical mind, with things that could have worked, but that is a waste of time. Trying to fix the past from things in the present, from a present notion, takes a lot of time. And it usually does not work out well.

This is when we start numbing ourselves with substances to get some relief. But it is only a temporary fix. Jung understood the psychological function of drugs in a different way than most. He saw they had the power to actually change what happens to the person's inner world. That they did more than simply mask psychic distress, they actually removed the cause of the distress for the time being. Chemical substances, he knew, worked at a deeper level, blurring the boundaries in the individual's inner world. When the splits were abolished, the fragmented worlds became merged. Once someone has experienced this sense of wholeness, they usually want to experience it again and again. But the wholeness that comes with intoxication is an illusory wholeness which dissolves when one sobers up. So the search to repeat the profound experience begins, and it is not one that is easily given up.

Commit to undertaking some form of meditation; commitment demands action. Yoga or a walking meditation might work better for you at first. There are plenty of guided meditations on YouTube if you want to start with those. Experiment and you will find one that works best for you. It does not have to be painful or complicated, just start with baby steps of quieting the body and mind. And then be open to what guidance comes through.

People might call their intuition, a Divine Thought, which is perfectly fine. It is still something that is not easily measurable or proven scientifically. Some people call this a gut feeling or an 'aha' moment. It is best not to get caught up in the name you choose or that another person chooses. It is the quiet voice inside of you, although some people sense, feel, or see rather than hear a voice. By practicing listening to your intuition, it will become second nature to you. It is based on the deeper emotions within you and can be used as a tool for guiding your life.

If you are a surface dweller and do not go deep enough to find out who you really are, you only react to life, never knowing that there is something deeper going on within yourself. This is like everything is stimulated by the outside, by the outside observation. Keeping up with the Jones' is typical of being a surface dweller. You cannot go deep enough inside to gather the information that would be beneficial to you. The evidence is that you only lead a reactionary and superficial life.

This type of living will only bring you chaos, drama, more pain, more denial, and suffering. You will only be the B actor, never rising above to your authentic self. You will probably listen to your mind as it tells you that you don't need to meditate, it won't work, it sounds stupid, you have the best ideas or whatever. But pride is a poison that will keep you from having the openness and humility to try something new. This type of scenario is just you fighting with yourself. Can you see that?

Increasing your intuition or being able to hear the quiet voice within takes discipline and time. In all probability, you are not going to be able to do it the first time. But everyone is capable of doing this; we all can access the wisdom of the universe. Some people are just better able to have clear intuition more than likely because they have been developing it for many years. When you are accessing this information, the evidence and indicators will be that you are calmer, and your life starts working better for you.

The irony is that when you give up some level of control over your life and leave it to a higher source, you will gain better control over managing your life. The more anyone tries to be in complete control over manifesting everything in their lives, the more exhausted they will be. Life can be much more effortless when you allow your life to unfold. The universe has a much bigger plan for you than anything you could imagine!

Most experts agree there are many benefits of practicing meditation. It will lower your stress levels and help you to gain control over your emotions. Meditation will help you be more present in your life, which helps you become more aware of who you are and what your purpose is. This helps you to accept yourself more and to be happier, and you will actually have more compassion for others too. Many schools are now incorporating meditation as a form of time out instead of detention for their students.

I resisted meditation for years. Whenever I did try it, my mind started with the list of everything I needed to do that day. So, I would quit and go and complete my list! I was always happy to finish my list of things to do, but I never got to experience the real benefits of meditation. Now I crave the time alone and the quiet time. My life is less hectic but more fulfilled. My relationships are better, and I have no desire to control everyone and anyone. I only wish I would have started sooner, but I did not know the reasons for quieting the mind and listening to spirit. I thought I had to do it all.

The best thing that happened to me after I started meditating was that I consistently felt calm no matter what the day would bring me. I could remain relaxed and balanced even if everyone around me were losing their composure. I also came to realize that there was a whole world other than the physical that I could sense and feel. There were different dimensions, and meditation was the key for me to experience something bigger than myself. Life started to make sense to me.

I used to become bored so quickly, which often got me into trouble I was not looking for. When I started meditating, I spent hours inside of myself. I was never bored because the levels of myself are so exciting, and there is always something to learn.

Simple 5-minute meditation: Set timer

Place both feet flat on the floor and both hands comfortably in your lap. Take a few deep breaths to get grounded and settled.

Now start breathing rhythmically. (count to 4 while breathing in; count to 4 breathing out)

Only focus on your breath. If your mind starts to wander, bring your focus back to your breath.

Notice any thoughts that come up and then go back to counting your breaths; in and out.

When the timer goes off, slowly open your eyes and focus on something around you.

Meditation 2: Record and playback while meditating

Place both feet flat on the floor and both hands on your lap.
Sit up straight and take a deep breath in . . . . and slowly let it out.
Close your eyes and imagine the number 3 . . . .
Now imagine the number 2 . . . .
And finally, imagine the number 1 . . . . .
As the number 1 disappears, take another deep breath in . . . . .
and slowly let it out.
Listen to your breath.
Listen to it go in . . . . . and out
And again, listen to it go in . . . . . and let it out.

Feel your body relaxing.
Feel your feet relax . . .
Feel your legs relax . . .
Feel your back relax . . .
Feel your arms relax. . .
Feel your neck relax . . .
And finally . . . feel your face relaxing.

Now imagine something that you feel grateful for.
Feel this gratitude in your heart center.
Imagine that this gratitude fills the room you are in.
Fill your entire space with gratitude.
Remember that feeling and keep it. . . .

Now imagine the number 3 again . . .
Imagine the number 2 again . . .
Imagine the number 1 again . . .
Take a deep breath in . . . and let it out.
Slowly open your eyes.

Limiting beliefs create a breakdown in your life experience. They live in your brain, and you know that everything your mind tells you is not valid. If you are running on misinformation and false beliefs, the end result will always be the same. When you are willing and open, you are allowing for a virgin Divine Thought to be heard. Make room for something awesome to happen, for a miracle to occur. Allow for at least a shift in your perception, which is a miracle. Let your spirit and soul be in charge of your life, not your mind.

Allow this Divine Wisdom to lead your decisions and your life. It is called soul searching for a reason. You are going deep within to find answers, and this is how you will integrate your spirit body with your mind and emotions. No longer will you be fragmented and/or compartmentalized and running on emotions that are out of control. No longer will you be unaware of why you are doing something and the link it has to your past. You will start to become whole and present, living in the moment from a place of joy.

In the beginning, your mind will rationalize away the magic that shows up at your door. Learn to trust yourself. Trust is a straight line. There are no crooked lines in it. There is a whole lot of freedom waiting to express itself through your trust. It is only insane to keep using your distorted ideas and think they are going to work this time. Put out the lifeline to your higher self and ask for guidance. It will come.

JOURNAL

MY 'AHA' MOMENT IN LIFE WHEN I HEARD A VOICE GUIDING ME.

WHEN I TRUSTED THAT VOICE AND LISTENED TO IT, THIS HAPPENED.

WHEN I DID NOT TRUST MY INTUITION, THIS HAPPENED.

MY WEEKLY MEDITATION INSIGHT:

HOW IS MY BODY RESPONDING TO MEDITATION?

HOW IS MY MIND RESPONDING TO MEDITATION?

CHAPTER FIVE

Become The Hero Of Your Story

One who looks outside, dreams, one who looks inside, awakes.
Carl Jung

If you are operating out of your mind and emotions, thereby reacting to life as it happens to you, you can never rise above the chaos to become the hero of your story. You cannot be the main star as you are too busy blaming others, feeling self-pity, or trying to keep up with all the chaos around you. You will only be an extra in your story. These are the people who are background filler for film and T.V. episodes.

Extras show up to the set and get placed around in the background by the director. They don't have much to do. It is easy work, but it can also become quite dull or frustrating. Most of the actors playing an extra actually have/had aspirations to play a leading role. Many probably think they could do as good a job in the lead role if only someone gave them a chance. Maybe they are right, but not everyone was born to be a star in a film or television show.

All of you, however, were born to be the star of your own story. The only thing it takes is courage. The courage to go within and investigate yourself. What is courage? Courage is a door opener. It is an attitude. If you have fear, try 'acting' fearless until the courage comes in and takes hold of you. If your anxiety is about sharing a deep secret about yourself, how would you feel if you were able to do it? Imagine it and feel it in every cell of your body. Imagine the freedom it would unlock in your soul.

Introspection is an art when you start taking responsibility. It takes a lot of courage to look at your responsibility in life. What was your part in it? This is the time to only look at yourself. What are you afraid of? When does self-pity enter your world? Courage is a demonstration working through your fear, in spite of your fear. It is a place of resolve that you can make go forward despite the obstacle. Fear is a corrosive agent as far as courage is concerned because it can be distractive and destructive.

I was blocked when it was time to do some inventory of myself. I did not want to write down anything. But I realized that made me stuck, my resistance was the only thing in the way. So I started reflecting and writing down the aspects of my life I avoided. It was painful, but it was also freeing. The commitment is what made me do it, so I summoned the courage to move forward. I needed it badly, and now I felt the urgency of not failing. Freedom was my reward and the ability to look at things from a rational point. I did not have to feel like a victim anymore. I gained power over my life.

Sometimes you have experiences you never get to fully resolve because you don't want to feel those feelings again. It becomes too overwhelming and scary to revisit those places. You might feel too much shame to admit your responsibility for aspects of your life. But our flaws and wounds are where we are more alike than not. It takes vulnerability and acceptance to admit your shortcomings. There are no perfect people in the world, only those people who might think they are relatively perfect!

Everyone also has experiences where in spite of their fear, they went forward, and they were the hero of their journey. Usually, the negative outcome is never as bad as you might have imagined. Often the positive result is more rewarding than most things you have done. Sometimes it takes courage just to do the right thing. It takes courage not to do the easy thing and to push yourself to try new things. After a while, your confidence will return, and you will be able to walk through stuff that makes you feel uncomfortable.

Fear can make you do irrational things, things that are not beneficial to you. Fear distorts your reality. What happens when your reality is distorted? Frustration comes in. You start feeling inadequate. You start measuring through your mind about who you are. That is a distortion right there. That attitude undermines any success you could have. Fear controls the outcome.

Fear is just your own energy that is filtered through beliefs systems out of alignment with your true, authentic self. If you behave in a manner that you want your reality to reflect, you can move through the fear. When you move through the jagged edges of resistance, you can tap into a bit of courage along the way. Courage actually builds upon itself, and you will find that you have more and more when you act upon it.

When you use courage, you start to become your own hero. It's when you can go inside of yourself and pull something out. You might say," I can make this shot." Even if you don't make it, you were able to take a chance using courage. Your buried pain often limits your courage. Examine your ideas, your emotions, and your attitudes. What shaped them? Why do you react strongly to certain things? Are your feelings all over the place?

When an actor lands a role, the real work begins for him/her. He will read the script many times and start investigating who the character really is beyond the story and the written words. There are more questions not answered in a script than are in plain view. In this intense examination, great actors will journal and write down answers to questions such as: What happened to me as a child? How do I feel about the other characters in the film? What are my fears? Who hurt me? What do I really want? What do I believe in?

This is the background story to help them portray a multi-faceted character instead of a one-dimensional character. This is the only way to understand the role and act authentically fully. The pages of the investigation will fill up many pages, just as your investigation into yourself will fill up many pages. You will start to find answers that will surprise you if you go deep enough.

When you start investigating your life, your attitudes, your beliefs, your emotions, our behavior, and your perceptions, you will unlock the mysteries of why your life is the way it is. You will unlock the potential for a better experience. You will start to see how your hopes, dreams, and wishes have the possibility of becoming a reality. This is how you will become whole again. How you will integrate your mind, body, and spirit.

My father never accepted me, and after he died, I finally dared to write him a letter and tell him how I felt. After I got accepted into USC to study law, he said, "Well, it's not Harvard." When I bought a house, he said, "Well, it will do for now," after he saw it. When I purchased a used Porche in beautiful condition and with low miles, he said, "Well, it's not new." The only time he praised me was when I bought cocaine. My father died from cocaine addiction. Now I am on Skid Row working on my addiction. I ended up losing everything, sold my car and house, which I loved. I realize all the pain I have been carrying around because of his rejection. I felt so free after I wrote the letter that I was even able to laugh about it all. That surprised me so much. I wish I had the courage years ago to confront my pain.

Your other choice is to live from the fear and pain, to live from your wounds and limiting beliefs. The mere act of moving forward through the fear will tend to diminish the fear. If you keep thinking about fear, it seems to magnify it more and more. You then become stuck on the Fear Channel!

Try examining what the worst thing possible that could happen if you..., if this happens..., if someone finds out..., if you don't succeed..., if you fail..., if your anger comes out..., if your relationship breaks up..., if you actually did do something wrong...., if you did not accomplish your goal..., or if your shame becomes overpowering.

If you push parts of yourself away from that you don't love and hide certain negative elements of you from others, you might succeed for many years. But, it becomes exhausting to keep this game up. You will become fragmented. You will become ill. Your body will break down. The secrets will become visible to many of the people you are trying to fool. Your mind will start obsessing about how to keep up the façade and what will happen if you are not successful.

This is what it means to be stuck. You cannot be present in your own body and space. If you are not present, you are not aware of much about you. Who are you really? What parts of you are not being accepted by you? Nothing can be brought to the surface to be healed. You will continuously be in a battle with yourself and not feel fulfilled no matter what good comes into your life.

To get out of your self-imposed HELL, you are going to have to see it. You are going to have to take a hard look at yourself, and this takes a great deal of courage. When you start seeing your coping mechanisms, you are on the right track. There is nothing wrong with using coping mechanisms when you are growing up. It might be the only way you think you can survive and come out less broken. But these coping mechanisms start becoming a hindrance as you become an adult. They start interfering with you becoming the best version of yourself.

Part of your introspection will be to identify your coping mechanisms and to ask if they are working for you today. If they are not working for you, you can better choose to use them or hopefully to not use them. This awareness brings in a new level of free-will choice. When that happens, identify how that feels in your body. You have just shifted your consciousness and integrated a part of yourself to start being whole.

Everyone has fragmentation, distortions, and dysfunction within their lives and families. It is just the nature of our human species over many generations. Fragmentations and distortions cause us to lose our relationship with our true selves. The healing process is not easy and is not fast and smooth. Expect your distortions and fragmentations to be in the hundreds, not ten or twenty. It will definitely feel overwhelming at times during your healing process, but you will start to see positive results from the very beginning.

One of the main reasons we don't want to go within and investigate ourselves is that it will most certainly precipitate a change in our lives. So, we do not want to change, we resist it. We become afraid that we will lose people and things that we love or have grown accustomed to. We fear losing our connections to others. We fear the unknown and most importantly, the 'what ifs' of the unknown. We fear being out of control of our future and bad or negative experiences. We fear losing peace and happiness.

Usually, you get to the point of where the pain of staying is more than the pain of changing. The cost-benefit of changing is better than staying in old outworn patterns of behavior. Just like the main character in any good story or film, our lives are about transforming and changing. The benefits, on the other side far outweigh the benefits of staying stuck. We can easily see it in films, and we root for the main character to take that chance, make the difficult choice that will inevitably cause pain, suffering, and build their character. We want the protagonist to look fear in the face and move through it.

At the end of the film, the protagonist can do something that he was unable to do at the beginning of the film. This is called his character arc, and his life is forever changed for the better. He has new skills and a new outlook on life. He can never go back to the way he was before, nor would he want to. He has become more whole, more integrated with his best version on himself. We feel satisfied leaving the movie theater, and we even feel a sense of accomplishment of witnessing this with another human being, albeit through the fantasy of film.

We need to admit our fears and the deeper meaning behind the fears concerning other people. This takes vulnerability and courage from the depths of your soul. And it will be gut-wrenching at times because it is coming from a deep level within that perhaps has not been touched before. But once that part of you has been chipped away, there will be a lightness of being and less fragmentation. You don't know yourself until you start seeing your value. If you don't ask the questions, you won't get the answers.

After I had been busted with a rock in my glove, I had to dig deep to discover my courage. I went to court, and the judge believed in recovery. I did not know what recovery was. The fear and uncertainty of what was going to happen to me were intense. I would go back to prison if I did not go into recovery, but I did not know if I could stop using. But I also knew that I did not want to go back to prison. That place I did know, and I did not like it. It took all the courage I could muster to overcome all my fears to start the road down my path to recovery. There are always fears that come up during the recovery process too. It permeates our lives every day. The emotional fear of not being good enough or not being as bad as you can imagine. The fear of 'what is going to happen to me?'. Am I going to survive tomorrow? The fear of the dark and the quiet. The most important thing was that I was able to move forward and to do something different. It was one of the best decisions of my life! My life improved day by day, year by year, and drastically over the 18 years that I have been sober.

For years and years, I saw no point in looking deep within myself to investigate old wounds and traumas. After all, my childhood past of sexual abuse was far in my past. I forgave my father and decided that I did not have too many after-effects from it. I had many successes in my life and even deep, meaningful relationships. But I realized I did not dig very deep, and I was not open to what I did not know. Although I had wrapped it up in a nice neat package and could skim the surface of it, when I was brave enough to dig deeper, I realized that I had become a people pleaser as a form of coping. By the way, I was propelled deeper when I developed intestinal problems, and a holistic practitioner suggested I look at some deep emotional wounds. At first, I thought he was mistaken!

But then, a small voice inside prompted me to listen. I realized my people pleasing had even become a compulsion. In other words, I was addicted to pleasing and helping other people. That coping mechanism was outdated and did not serve me well at all. It was a relief to stop doing it, and I think people like me better today than in the past because I am more authentic. But the only thing that matters is that I like myself more.

Say out loud to yourself, "I am courageous. I am courageous. I am courageous." Now, wait. Sit quietly and listen. There is a part of yourself that will never lie to you. Listen to the small voice.

When we start investigating our lives, our attitudes, our beliefs, our emotions, our behavior, and our perceptions, we will unlock the mysteries of why our life is the way it is. We will unlock the potential for a better experience. We will start to see how our hopes, dreams, and wishes,= have the possibility of becoming a reality. This is how we will become whole again; how we will integrate our minds, bodies, and spirits.

The greatest act of courage is to be and own all that we are without apology, without excuses, and without any masks to cover the truth of who we truly are. And remember that courage is contagious; others will follow our lead and feel a sense of freedom to express their true nature too! Courage is not about the end game; it is going from failure to failure without losing your enthusiasm!

We have all used courage to get out of sticky situations to move forward in life. Courage comes in place of the observation to propel action. The inspection afterward shows us the positive consequences of our bravery.

I got my cosmetology license in 1982. I never had my own business because I was afraid of failure. I chose to only work for other people, and I had a successful career. I was offered my own salon, and I even had the money, $10,000. I did not take it because I was too afraid. Today, I wonder how my life would be different if I dared to follow my dreams.

Fear traps us in insanity, we don't want to try something new. The fear of doing something new, fear of failure. Yoda was a Jedi Master in the Star War's Films and was very wise because of his connection to the Force (Source). He said, "Fear is the path to the dark side. Fear leads us to anger...anger leads to hate...hate leads to suffering."

First, acknowledge your fear. What is keeping you trapped? If you don't acknowledge your weaknesses, they capture you in the most unexpected times. Fear will always have a conversation with you, directing you to places you don't want to go. Those places tend to be the same thing over and over, like a deep gouge in the road. Use courage as the fuel to keep exploring yourself. This is the way to get out of the rut you are in.

As in any film, there is a call to action for our hero. This is an invitation to start the journey and inevitable transformation. And just like the characters in films, it takes a great deal of courage to begin any journey. Remember Luke Skywalker in *Star Wars*? His call to action was to go out into the world and believe in himself. Dorothy's call to action in *The Wizard of Oz* was to transform her beliefs of not valuing home. Rose's call to action in *Titanic* was to take ownership of her own life. The hero in the film always rises up to meet the challenge. Become the hero of your story, rise up to meet your challenges and obstacles, and start today.

JOURNAL

HOW HAS FEAR TURNED ME INTO A VICTIM?

HOW HAS FEAR CONTROLLED MY LIFE?

IF I COULD BE COURAGEOUS, WHAT WOULD I DO?

IF I KNEW I WOULD BE SUCCESSFUL, WHAT WOULD I DO?

WHEN I WAS COURAGEOUS, I DECIDED TO...

WHAT IS THE GREATEST IDEA OF MYSELF I CAN CREATE TODAY?

HOW CAN I DEMONSTRATE BEING COURAGEOUS TODAY?

MY BIGGEST FEAR IS...

WHAT WOULD IT TAKE FOR ME TO HAVE MORE COURAGE?

CHAPTER SIX

Shoot-Out At OK Corral

The gunfight at the OK Corral in Tombstone, Arizona in 1881 was one of the more memorable moments of history, and it only lasted 30 seconds. A lot of damage was done in those few seconds between lawmen and the outlaws known as the cowboys. It has been immortalized in many movies, including *Frontier Marshal, Gunfight at the OK Corral, Tombstone,* and *Wyatt Earp.* While the gunfight is legendary and we seem to never tire of seeing a good one in our films, most of the shoot-outs we experience in our modern day are done with words or tweets.

Do you continually find yourself in a shoot-out with other people? If you see that their 'gun' is loaded, and they are firing, do you shoot back? Do you run for cover and shoot from behind the rock? Is it too difficult to resist the temptation to fire off some rounds of your own, rounds of hurtful words or actions? Words are like projectiles; they can wound us. Since you can never take back hurtful words, there are wounded and dying in the aftermath. The clean-up is not easy. There is usually some form of regret to deal with too. Of course, having a shoot-out is a metaphor for having a dramatic confrontation or argument with someone else.

If there is a lot of evidence of Mr. Chaos and Lady Drama showing up in your life, first look to what causes you to have resentment. What is resentment? *To feel angry or bitter about something. To feel strongly; discomfort to the mind. Disappointment.* If your immediate thought is that you hold no resentments, let's imagine someone you used to have resentment for. You might say you have forgiven them, however; if they come around and you feel strange, you are still holding onto that resentment. Your mind can easily play games with you while you pretend that the bitterness is gone, but your feelings will never lie.

Take time to investigate and journal about your hurtful experiences in life thoroughly. Experience is a great teacher, but you must check in with it and go deep within to acknowledge your feelings to find the truth. Your feelings are the barometer to what needs to heal. You are not a bad person or wrong if you still have anger and resentment. Your feelings are valid and only a holding place from where the healing can begin, if and when you are ready.

On some level, we all know that forgiveness is the better choice rather than holding on to resentment and anger. But forgiveness does not have an ON and OFF switch within us. To expect that we should be able to flip the switch and then let go of all the resentments we have had for years is unrealistic and not helpful. We end up feeling bad about ourselves for yet another thing we are unable to do. We can dig in our heels even more and justify why that other person does not deserve our forgiveness. This is not helpful either.

When I started my spiritual journey, I did not realize how I was so compartmentalized. I had suppressed so much of the trauma and abuse over the years. This worked for me as a kid, kind of like a survival mode to keep coping with life. I could not even access the anger and resentment I felt at being ridiculed or made fun of. Everything was tucked away so I would not have to deal with something I was incapable of dealing with as a kid. So, when I was older, I thought I had forgiven those people. After all, I did not feel angry or resentful. Forgiveness became a mental process because that was what I was supposed to do, being on a spiritual path. Only when I was willing to go back and address the traumas, was I able to access the truth of the matter. Now I look back and laugh at how I was fooling myself. I 'thought' I was so spiritual, advanced, and kind, but that was a big lie. There is no quick and easy way to forgiveness or to becoming whole again.

Memories demand your attention, like a neglected, needy child, always pulling at your sleeve. Memories can be stuffed for only so long. Then they will start creeping up on you, only to have you push them away again and again. But then physical symptoms can appear 'out of nowhere.' It's as if your inner child is saying, 'pay attention to me.' Usually, when the pain or symptoms become too much to ignore, we start to pay attention. But we might not know how to connect all the dots from the emotional trauma to the physical pain and disease happening in the body. We might not realize that our panic attacks are related to years of unprocessed emotions.

First, look at what happened to you. Then take that deeper to what you imagine was taken from you. Was it your innocence? Your childhood? Your dignity and self-respect? Your sense of security or trust in another human being or the world? Your confidence? Your sense of safety or belonging? Your happiness? Your health? Your ability to function in a healthy way? Your dreams? Did you stop believing in yourself? How did you change for the worse? What hardships did you endure because of the trauma or incident? What was the trauma you went through because of the event? What was lost that you think might never return?

Once you have identified the many layers of your trauma through journaling, drawing, or speaking it out loud to another person, the healing process can begin within you. Remember, you cannot heal something that you are not aware of. You must take responsibility for your own healing because if you wait for the other person to ask for forgiveness, you could be waiting for a very long time. Life would be easier if the person who has wronged you apologizes, begs forgiveness, and promises never to do it again. Sometimes we justify not apologizing until the person who has wronged us asks us to forgive them, but the end result is the same. We are filled with resentment until we take responsibility to heal it.

I only had rebellion and resentment as my tools to heal myself. But instead of improving myself, I dug myself deeper into a pit of hopelessness. I became aware that I was being damaged by holding onto the resentment and ill will towards others. I realized that by letting go, slowly, I was gaining some freedom in my life. I did not want to keep lugging around that trunk of unresolved hurt. When I shined the spotlight on it, it released some of its grip on me. I started to realize that resentment was part of the past and not the present moment where I tried to live now. Every day my goal is to live in the present moment, free from the shackles of anger or resentment.

Healing ourselves is an inside job. It all begins with the question. Many times, the question is not what you would have expected or planned. Many times, the answer is not what you would have expected or anticipated. But when the process creates that moment that feels like time stands still, when a lightbulb goes off in your mind, or when it makes you pause and take a deep breath, it is a Divine moment of grace. You will never be the same again. A shift has occurred and a reset for starting over from a new place of perception and awareness. That is part of what the healing process feels and looks like.

Five years into my recovery, I attended a meeting and heard another man speak about his relationship with his mother in such a loving and supportive way. I asked myself, "I wonder why I don't have that kind of a relationship with my mother?" Later, when I was at the donut shop, I saw the answer. It flashed before me. That day when I was four years old and the police came to take my father away. My mother had made the call. My father had not done anything that I could see to justify him being taken out of my home, away from me. It was the first time I realized I blamed her for not having my father around very much. I had never connected all the dots before, how I carried this resentment toward her for many years. I cried many tears of pain, relief, and joy.

The best place to start is to forgive yourself. Forgive yourself for anything and everything you have judged. If you have unfavorably compared yourself to another, forgive yourself. If you have criticized yourself, forgive yourself. Many times, we abuse ourselves worse than we would ever allow another human being to! Forgive yourself for the times you ingested anything less than healthy into your body. Forgive yourself for all the times you have played small, doubted your gifts and abilities, berated yourself, or were too afraid to act on an opportunity. Forgive yourself for all the mistakes you have made. Forgive yourself for all the times you sold out when you felt that money was more important than staying true to your character.

In the film, *The Hobbit, The Desolation of Smaug,* the characters had to go through the Milkwood Forest to get to their destination. There was no shortcut, no easier way to their destination. It had to be done no matter how they felt about it. This is a metaphor for our lives as well. We must go through some muck and mire to clear away all that is not needed in our spiritual/physical/emotional/mental transformation. When everything starts getting cleared out, it is painful. It is painful to relive memories we thought we would never have to look at again. It is painful to let go of limiting beliefs, false illusions, resentments, lies, distortions, and our masks that hide who we really are.

When we are living from our wounds, there will be resentment showing up on the set. Even though the past is done and there is nothing we can do about it, it has a strong hold on us. It is sending out subtle or not so subtle signals that will affect our behavior and attitudes. Resentment is running the show! Resentment takes away choice; we start reacting versus responding to situations. It is directing your life. It holds your personality hostage, and you are in bondage to yourself. Now the personality cannot develop with any kind of truth or authenticity. There are really no benefits to holding onto resentment and anger.

Forgiveness will not change what has happened to you. But it will most certainly change your future. But the process of forgiveness needs to be organic and dynamic. And it must start with healing yourself. You have the power to heal yourself no matter if the other person apologizes or acknowledges their wrongdoing. You have the ability to heal your wounds and traumas by first giving them some attention. What happened? What does your body need? What does your spirit need? What do you need to heal your emotions? What would your life look like if you were able to forgive everyone and anyone? How would your life be different?

I endured sexual abuse when I was a child, and it distorted my understanding of relationships and boundaries. I found myself continually choosing men who would cheat on me, lie about it, and eventually get caught. It became so tiring, feeling betrayed so often. I kept asking, "What is wrong with me? What am I doing wrong?" When I asked the then current boyfriend these questions, he answered, "You did not do anything wrong. I am at fault. I felt insecure and made these choices to feel better about myself." I realized that I was abusing myself by continually blaming myself for other people's bad behavior! I shifted. I started only to take responsibility for my shit. I realized that was all I was required to do, take responsibility for me and my behaviors. And that was the last time anyone cheated on me.

Let's imagine that the wound from being cheated on is betrayal and a lack of trust towards someone new. What would be needed to heal? To be able to trust again. Let's imagine that the next relationship is healthy and happy. You slowly start developing trust in both your decisions and in another person's character. By building that trust within, the resentment you had to your Ex starts to dissolve. When you think of him/her, the adverse reaction is not as strong. When you start healing, the resentment begins dissolving. You do have the power. Your healing does not need to start with the other person apologizing. You have the magic within you. You are wearing the red, ruby slippers; just take the first step.

Resentment sets up a modus operandi within the individual. It affects the personality, and you can become a bad actor without even being aware of it. You cannot be content, happy, fulfilled, or free because you are in bondage to yourself when the pattern of resentment takes over. It is a Jedi Mind Trick. You forget who you are, who you want to be, and where you were going. The denial becomes stronger if you believe you are immune to the negative patterns. Before long, you feel trapped with no exit strategy, full of isolation and self-pity.

> *I carried around a lot of resentment and anger, and I felt that was a good thing. I thought that it was a sort of body armor, protecting me from abusers. I thought it made me stronger and more formidable to others. I thought I could control what other people did to me this way. But I was wrong. I finally realized that when I carried the fight around with me, the only thing I created was more fight. When I started to let go of the resentments, I began to relinquish my need to control others too. I realized that I only had control over me and my reactions, but that surprisingly felt more powerful! I was then able to accept other people without trying to control or change them. Today, I rarely have chaos and drama, and I don't miss it one bit.*

The check-in becomes essential each and every day for the rest of your life. The check-in requires that we live in the present moment and are brutally honest with ourselves about our feelings with no judgment or editing to make them prettier. Otherwise, our life becomes a runaway train, and we hope there is no crash. There is an excellent chance that we might have a shoot-out with someone else, though. That is a reliable indicator that things might not be going along as well as you thought. It is time to reevaluate and to put our lives back in balance. When you are balanced, you have nothing but the present moment.

Your resentment can easily cloak itself with passive-aggressive communication and behavior. This is when you are not direct with expressing your thoughts and feelings. You might pout or make sarcastic remarks or throw out vague insults that are difficult to comprehend. You might agree to do something, but then not do it. You might procrastinate and be late for appointments. You might 'forget' to do something that you promised to do. A person might even appear to be agreeable, diplomatic, and supportive but are actually back-stabbing duplicitous and dishonest. There is a disconnect between what is said and what is done and an unwillingness to communicate in a healthy way. Underneath it all is deep resentment and anger that bubbles to the top and creates chaos.

If you are continually blaming others for your circumstances, always playing the victim card with your finger pointing outward, that is another good indicator that you are carrying around a lot of anger and resentment. Being a professional victim is not a good look. That is one rule when writing a great screenplay, never have your protagonist be a victim. No one wants to see it; no one wants to root for them to win. This victimhood behavior can easily lead to an addiction because of all the sympathy and attention it brings to you. Just repeating the stories of what everyone else has done to you will do nothing to heal your wounds,. And by holding onto that negative energy, you become corrupted, distorted, and unbalanced.

You might think that you hold no resentment toward anyone else, or that you are unaware of where your dissatisfaction lies. First, look to what triggers you to have a reaction. What caused a tender place inside of you to open up? What kind of bad memories seep out of the wound, asking for some attention? This is the place that needs healing and compassionate care. If anger and resentment toward someone else come up first, be careful not to play the blame game or fall into victimhood. This will take you on a roller coaster ride and distract your process of healing.

I thought I had forgiven this person for stealing from me. But when I heard that another person had taken something from them, I felt pure joy. I felt the sweet revenge and believed that karma had come knocking on their door. But this conflict of emotions also came up in me. If I really thought stealing was terrible, was it only a terrible thing when it happened to me? I realized I could and should not lose any outrage of taking from another, that if my values are not consistent, then something else is going on. In all honesty, I guess I had not forgiven that person. I laughed at how easily my mind was trying to trick me.

Forgiveness is a principle, a law for living. The quality of life based on principles like honesty, hope, faith, courage, integrity, willingness, patience, and forgiveness is much higher than living from the personality. The personality and mind are filled with inconsistencies. Principles never waiver. They are not mutable. The personality can be fickle. Principles before personality is a slogan for a healthier lifestyle.

I paid dearly for all the resentment I held onto against the police. Every time I saw the cops, I wanted to fight them. I thought, 'you are not going to make me do anything.' I fought them and got beat in the head with a baton. I did not learn at that time. The second time I was put in a choke hold and passed out. The third time, I was tasered six times, all with the same attitude, you can't make me do anything. I did not even know why I was fighting them; my resentment was buried so deep. My dad said to me, "Son, you are going to have to stop fighting the police. They are going to kill you." I stopped fighting the police, but it took many more years to get in touch with the reasons why I held onto so much resentment and anger. Looking back, I am lucky my resentment did not get me killed.

Resentment can act like a wild card, no easy way to channel it once it is embedded within you. It might start with someone speaking harshly to you and then morph into many other situations caused by the first resentment! The entrance wound and the exit wound might not be the same. It is always better to first start with the entry wound, but that might take days of journaling, meditation, and contemplation to go deep within. It might take months or years to get to the original wound finally. But when you do, it will stop governing your life.

How might you heal your lost innocence? It might be through learning how to be more child-like. What are most kids like? Creative, playful, curious, feeling like everything new is exciting! Feeling grateful for the smallest of things. Feeling a sense of wonder at the world and all there is around you. Spend some time with children, playing and talking to them to help remember what it feels like to be innocent again. Let go of time and any responsibilities for at least an hour while you play. Feel the pure joy they feel while playing and being silly. That spark is still within you, it has just been covered up. Learn to fan the flames of those qualities and have the discipline to play every week.

If your confidence was taken from you, what steps can you take to heal that within? Weed out anyone in your life who does not have your best interests at heart. Get rid of friends and family who criticize you or who cannot see the brilliance within you. Find people who love you more than you love yourself. When you have an excellent support team of 4 or 5 people, you can then start trying new things in your life. Share with your team how you need their support and kind words of encouragement. After your first accomplishment, set new goals. Reward yourself for your success! When you have people around that believe in you, you will start believing in yourself. You know the people who feed your soul because you feel good after your time with them.

Resentment becomes an agent for misperception and a lousy attitude, which then becomes terrible behavior. It becomes a lifestyle of nastiness. You can then become a haven for demonic thoughts, negative behavior, and a destructive lifestyle. It creates a cesspool which affects everything in your life. Even through your niceties, the nastiness seeps through. Your life is orchestrated by the resentment, you are living your life through a black veil of misperception. There is no brightness or light, everything is filtered through your lies. While the hatred and resentment are corroding you bit by bit, your clever mind justifies it.

Resentment places a wall between you and the other person. You believe you are protecting yourself, but in order to heal, you must find some level of compassion and empathy toward that person who has harmed you. This will create a connection with that person that we have walled off to 'protect' ourselves. Having empathy and compassion toward someone also cannot be forced. But all it takes is for the heart to open a little bit in order to feel how the perpetrator might feel. To maybe understand how life did not treat him/her reasonably either. To realize that they need healing too or they would not have acted so atrociously.

My father abused me when I was young, and this was so damaging to me. I felt a lot of anger and disgust toward him for the longest time. When I was older, I learned about my grandfather, his father. That man was a monster who was institutionalized for mental illness. He raped his daughters, beat his wife and children, and even shot at them all with a gun! He terrorized his whole family and had very few redeeming qualities if any at all. I shifted in that moment of seeing what my father went through. I realized he dealt with so much trauma and did not have the tools, education, or support team to become healthy and whole. He did not talk about it much until he was in his 80's and even then, with tears in his eyes. My compassion melted my anger and resentment. I only wanted him to be free from his pain.

Sometimes we hold onto resentment as a way of saying, "You cannot treat me this way!" This is a way to have a boundary with others, and if you have never had healthy boundaries, there can be a positive outcome as a consequence of your situation. Setting boundaries is a way to empower yourself and a healthy way to live life. It will also help you move from a victim consciousness (having no power) to one of empowerment. Practice communicating your expectations with others in a healthy way to ensure that you do not take responsibility for another's bad behavior. Eventually, you will come to realize that you don't need the resentment to hold onto your healthy boundary.

There are no perfect people in a film because we are not perfect. We have all watched a movie and fell in love with a character through all their flaws and imperfections. We can feel compassion and empathy toward another human being that has done some terrible things. It becomes more complicated if the injustice is done to us, but it is possible. And when you finally lift off the chains of resentment, you will feel free.

If you are willing to look at another person's behavior toward you as a reflection of the state of their relationship with themselves rather than a statement about your value as a person, then you will, over some time cease to react at all.

– Yogi Bhajan

JOURNAL

I AM NOT SURE I CAN EVER FORGIVE THIS PERSON(S).

IF I COULD RELEASE MY RESENTMENT, THIS IS HOW MY LIFE WOULD CHANGE.

IF I COULD LET GO OF ALL MY ANGER AND RESENTMENT, THIS IS HOW I WOULD FEEL.

HOLDING ONTO MY RESENTMENT BENEFITS ME BY...

ONE TIME WHERE I FORGAVE A PERSON WAS...

WHEN I FORGAVE SOMEONE, IT CHANGED THEIR LIFE BY...

WHEN I FORGAVE SOMEONE, IT CHANGED MY LIFE BY...

FORGIVING PEOPLE...

AM I ABLE TO ACCEPT THE HURTS AND TRAUMAS IN MY LIFE?

CHAPTER SEVEN

What Is Your Cover Story?

One of the ways you can become a bad actor is to show up to the set and try and control all aspects of the filming. Do you try and arrange the lights, move scenery, direct other actors and generally believe that life would be great if only other people would just do what you want and what you tell them to? But if you are completely honest with yourself, the show never comes off as you want it to and often it is a disaster. This can lead to anger, frustration, self-pity, and even isolation.

You become isolated because you want to control everything, and that will only work for so long with others. The only thing you are creating is a hostile environment. Then others kick you to the curb, or you get angry and take your wagon and toys and refuse to play with others. You want so desperately to try and make life operate like how you think it should. But, you never get a chance to live your life, because you have not taken time to get to know who you are when you are just reacting to life.

It is also interesting when you are so focused on trying to control others; usually, it's because you feel you have no self-control. Are your emotions under your control? NO. Are your behaviors under your control? NO. Your emotions are misfiring. You become unreasonable, irrational, and unreceptive to what might be good for you. You are dominated by a warped sense of reality, and you cannot trust your perceptions but are often in denial as to what is happening. Usually, it takes a crisis to allow us to move into a space of humility, a place where the distortion can be eradicated. The crisis takes away the clever factor and leaves a space that needs to be there. A crisis is an agent for change where you realize you no longer can be in control.

I was always trying to fix other people; my focus was outside of myself for most of the time. It made me feel good, and I would tell myself what a good person I was for trying to help other people. But many times, I was met with resistance and anger.

When people would leave, I blamed the person because they did not want to "improve themselves." It was when I started doing my internal work did I realize it was only a distraction so that I did not have to look at what I needed to do. The reality was that my life was not how I wanted it to be, so why was I qualified to tell anyone how to lead their life? The irony is, that when I focused on improving my life, I did not want to get distracted with another person's stuff!

Whether you are aware of it or not, there is a constant struggle going on if you are trying to control aspects of your life or other people. This takes a great deal of energy. It is also an unproductive use of your will because in all likelihood you will find yourself blaming others, feeling shame for yourself, and ruining relationships. You are not in touch with the reality of what is really going on, so, therefore, it is impossible to take responsibility for your part. This book is an invitation for you to throw several of your life-long concepts and beliefs out the window; stop knowing so much. It won't be easy but understand that your best thinking got you in the place you are now.

It might not have occurred to you before that you can simply let go of the control, and your life would run more smoothly. When we are in the flow of the universe, beautiful things begin to happen. This is a place of surrender which does not have to occur amid a crisis. It is a place of openness where you realize you don't have all the answers and you are not the one running the show, you are merely steering the boat.

This is the place where miracles happen, where you feel like Lady Luck has made a stop at your door, where the angels or the divine are answering your prayers. This is the place where you live from an open heart and feel the sense of well-being it brings to you. This is the place where your relationships improve because you relinquish control over another human being. This is the place where you feel calm as you trust that the universe supports you no matter what. And this is the place where you gain clarity and vision about universal truth and wisdom in order to lead your life in a healthy way.

When you relinquish control over outside things and other people, a trust that things are going to get better can start to emerge. When we start gaining confidence in our trust, faith develops. Humility, Trust, Faith, and Willingness are principles that need to be guiding your life. That is if you wish to lead a healthy life and create true happiness and joy from within. Principles are dynamic, not static. They inspire you to have a better story, and they can release you from patterns of destruction.

If you are feeling any sense of resistance to these words or the ideas, there is no willingness on your part. An open-minded person embraces taking chances, making mistakes, is free of illusions of guilt, doesn't mind what people think or say about them, and is willing to question everything.... even themselves. Some indicators and evidence of no willingness: You are not willing to challenge your old beliefs, you tend to discount anything new, you are stagnated or closed-minded, you feel stuck, you feel helpless and frustrated, and/or you make a lot of excuses and play the blame game (it is always someone else's fault).

This resistance can present itself in outlandish stories, rationalizations, defensiveness, and anger. But this is just a cover story, not the truth of what is really going on. It is not the truth of who you really are. There is a conflict going on inside of you, and you are resisting letting go of what you need to in order to change. The resistance and cover story are between the change and the old way of being. It is trying to hold onto something because the unknown is so scary.

> I was walking down the street and met a fellow who was supposed to be in recovery. I knew that because he was in one of my support groups that I was leading. I saw that he had a beer in his hand. I was not going to say anything, but he recognized me. He said, "It is my birthday. Oh, I am allowed to celebrate on my birthday." I still did not say anything. Then he paused a bit and added, "You know I don't drink!" That was his cover story. He did not want to acknowledge the facts, and he did not want anyone to correct him. And on some level, this made perfect sense to him while taking a sip of beer from the can!

Your true and authentic self is just under all this cover story waiting to shine its brilliant light. Within each one of us lies a deep reservoir of creativity, ideas, inspiration, and a sense of just 'knowing' which will give our lives direction and purpose. Your life is simply a reflection of how much truth is present in it. Living from truth will cause your life to expand and allow you to live in a heightened sense of awareness. While your true self might be temporarily obscured from you, it can never be destroyed. It is waiting for you to uncover all the magnificence that it is.

The only way to uncover and discover your authentic, true self is to go through your dark side. It gets ugly when you have to admit your responsibility, even to yourself. There is always an unwillingness to look at our part, still some resistance. The hardest thing is to look in the mirror and admit our part because then we would have to change. The pathway to break free is to look honestly at ourselves. Passivity is our enemy. Denial is our enemy. Stubbornness is our enemy. Perpetrating a fantasy is our enemy. If there is no transparency, there is no hope. Your dark side is not going away, it is just your job to bring more light into your life.

In the climate of denial, there is no content in the mind to reference. You are working from impulses, reactions, and emotional instability. When you can put forth your intention and attention, your addiction can be tempered. When you become conscious of the resistance, you start living in the change. Change becomes willingness. You stop listening to the clever mind; you start looking at things that would be healthy for you. The brain now has something new to fixate on. The real cause and effect of your actions become clear. When you stop ingesting the substance, you start to come out of the influence of your mind. Choice has a chance to enter the room.

I remember one time I was on the bus, and my body started sending out signals that I needed to use. By this time in my life, I wanted to stop using so bad that it would bring me to my knees, begging for help. But, that day, shortly after asking, I got off the bus, and I bought some more stuff. There was always this resistance to change, the willingness could not operate even if I had the desire. When the substance came around, there was no control and therefore, no choice. The willingness only came after a major crisis, which was the threat of going to prison again.

Resistance becomes a hotbed of lies, and you become a hot mess too with the cry of, "I am just fine the way I am!" Fear is the underlying emotion driving your story. But fear is just your own energy that is filtered through belief systems out of alignment with your true self, your authentic self. When you act on terror, it creates more and more resistance. Your feelings can guide you into a realization and awareness of your resistance to change. When you stop creating your cover story and instead sit with the emotions and feelings that are coming up, most importantly, the fear.

Remember, in any film story, the protagonist has some resistance at the beginning where he/she does not want to embark on the journey being laid out before them. It is human nature to resist on some level, but when it becomes the dominating pattern controlling your life, you will become stagnant. You will not be able to grow and transform. You will not be able to thrive despite the challenges in your path. The distortions will need to become even more elaborate, the longer you hold onto this fear and resistance. Your cover story will start to have holes, and you cannot keep telling the same lies over and over.

The fear will trap us because we are afraid of losing the part of our lives that we like. What if I lose my friends? What if I lose my husband? What if I lose my wife? What if I lose my family? Most humans are quite fearful of being alone and losing their connections with their loved ones. Some have isolated themselves from family but are afraid of losing the community they are a part of now, the community they are comfortable in. We crave meaningful connection as human beings and realize how fragile it can be.

When you are smoking crack, you have a culture and community that you are a part of. It is this same community and friends that can lure you back into some bad habits you are trying to kick. It can keep you from having the willingness to change. The fear has already set your life path, doing foolish things. Fear creates a false sense of reality. False Evidence Appearing Real is the acronym for fear. The fear and resistance keep us from asking the right question. Operating from these old patterns will get us pretty much more of the same. The same test pattern will come up, like the old test pattern that came up on the television at 10 or 11 at night in the '70s.

But it is the sense of community which can aid the recovery process too. There becomes a force higher than you, the new community, and family you have been craving. There were some drug studies done with rats which were called Rat Park. One group of rats was put into a beautiful idyllic setting with other rats, complete with toys, nature, lots of stimulation, plenty of food, and companionship. One group was isolated into lone cages with no stimulation or companionship.

The first group would actually refuse the drugs when given an option, they instead chose water to drink. The second group would always prefer to drink the water with drugs in it.

Recreating those same circumstances is impossible with human beings because we have many stressors to contend with each and every day. We will have traumas, dramas, setbacks, and other challenges, and nothing can protect us from most of it. But what the takeaway from the experiment is, is that a sense of connection and community affects us profoundly and positively. That these elements seem necessary to heal our wounds, help us maintain healthy choices, and hopefully even keep us from going down a dead-end street that we have been on before.

I used to say, "I am a nonconformist," that was my rebel cry. But the stakes got higher, and the AA house was the last on the block for me, my last hope. Even then, I resisted a part of the group and what I was supposed to say at the beginning. I held onto a little bit of resistance because I refused to say that I was an alcoholic. Instead, after my name, I said, "I am a human being." But something changed when I finally said, "I am an alcoholic." When I decided to try someone else's idea because my ideas were not working that well, my life got better. I can laugh now at my distorted view of non-conforming. I tried to the bitter end to hold onto some idea that I was not like everyone else and that I did not need anyone else! My Willingness was a life changer.

It's funny how Willingness shows up on the set. Many times, we can be so stubborn that it takes something to shake us up. We can find ourselves in a situation where our behaviors do not serve us anymore. We start to surrender to the idea that change must come. A real assessment comes without self-pity. A truth of the situation emerges, an acceptance, and a surrendering. Willingness is a point of surrender when the ego cannot find another idea or option other than to kill itself. When the excuses, justifications, and rationalizations cannot continue, a surrender happens.

Some people have to be badly mangled for the solutions to have an opening. If you are closed minded, there are no options. You only want to work with ideas that you think are true. Most people want to be right and will give you a cover story of why things should be the way they are. Sometimes the story does not even make sense. Your closed mind can trick you into believing anything, it is that powerful.

The greatest story ever told is told by an addict. Nothing in Hollywood can compare with the creativity involved in their experiences nor in their cover story. No matter your experience, they will come up with one that is bigger, better, more outlandish, and more hysterical than yours. Does not matter how believable it is, they own that story, lock, stock, and barrel. Even if you try and pierce holes in their cover story, they will come up a hundred reasons why it is true. It is their story, and they are sticking to it!

I was turning 18 soon and could inherit about $18,000 from my trust fund. The only problem was that I was in a bad place, and my mom knew the money would not go to a good cause. It was supposed to pay for my college education. She fought me for a while, but eventually gave up and handed the money over to me. I went through it in about three months. I was buying meth every other day for my friends and me. After the money was gone, I told everyone that it was stolen from me. I ultimately played the victim card with an elaborate story that kept changing. I thought it was believable, but later, my aunt told me no one believed me.

Having a cover story is like having a costume on all the time. You might have quick wardrobe changes if your cover story changes from situation to situation, from one group of friends to another. You can be really clever with the rapid changes and not even question if what you are doing is healthy. But with so many variations there is sure to be a wardrobe malfunction sooner or later. One part of your hidden self might seep out somewhere where it does not belong. Your mask covering part of your true self might accidentally slip off.

I used to have several different groups of friends, none of them knew each other. It felt perfectly reasonable for me to have 'work' friends, 'party friends,' 'old friends,' 'new friends,' 'spiritual friends,' and family. I never questioned why my friends were not integrated with each other until someone pointed out that "I was very compartmentalized." I started investigating the statement because I felt there was some element of truth to that. I felt the fear of not feeling like I could be myself within specific groups. I felt the need to be accepted and liked. Then I questioned why I would want to be friends with anyone if I could not be honest around them. It was the beginning of my journey toward becoming authentic. Today I have the freedom of being myself, and if someone cannot accept me, we just are not meant to be friends.

Many times, we hold onto a firm core belief. When we are presented with evidence that works against that belief, this new evidence cannot be accepted by us. This is called cognitive dissonance. You might feel it is so essential to protect your core belief that you will rationalize, ignore, and even deny anything that does not fit with your core belief. Be aware of this extreme reaction and feeling within as you are reading this book and journaling. Go deeper into the fear and resistance.

My sister borrowed money from our mom to buy a car. She claims she is a good person and a Christian. She even sings in the choir at church. But when it came time to pay my mom back, she disconnected from our family. She started inventing all these reasons why she does not have to pay the money back. Her excuses did not make a lot of sense to anyone but her, I guess. But the real problem is that her words and behaviors do not match up to me. There is a real perversion of reality going on in her mind. Our family is left as collateral damage, it is so hurtful.

The process of finding your true and authentic self is not really finding yourself; you are not lost. It is merely uncovering the real you that is buried beneath old patterns of thinking and programming from schools, churches, and family. It is the real person, uncluttered from cultural conditioning, other people's opinions, and incorrect conclusions that you came to as a child that created limiting beliefs you have been living from for many years. When you realize that you have been on lockdown for most of your life, you will be ready to break free. Underneath all that useless garbage is the real you, just waiting to break those chains of confinement.

When you are living from your authentic self, you will have the attitude of, "what you see is what you get." You will not be living from a place of fear, insecurity, or make-believe. You will not have a need to wear any mask or to live from a façade of truth. You will gain the freedom to explore all aspects of yourself, throwing out what does not serve you anymore. You get a chance to breathe and to just be present in all areas of your life. To live a life of presence is the greatest gift you can give yourself.

JOURNAL

WHAT COVER STORY HAVE I USED IN THE PAST?

WHAT COVER STORY AM I STILL USING?

WHERE DO I FEEL I CAN BE AUTHENTIC?

WITH WHOM DO I FEEL I CAN BE AUTHENTIC? WHY?

WHY DO I FEEL I NEED A COVER STORY?

IF I COULD JUST BE MYSELF WITHOUT ANY JUDGEMENT FROM OTHERS, HOW WOULD I FEEL?

HOW AM I JUDGING MYSELF?

CHAPTER EIGHT

Who Showed Up On The Set Today?

In any film production, it is essential to always come to the set prepared and ready to film your scene. Anything less than the best such as knowing your lines, being in character, being professional, and being on time costs the production company a lot of wasted money. When you get hired, the producers are depending on you to fulfill your commitment. They don't want to be surprised if and when you show up to the set having a nervous breakdown (the worst case) or even not knowing your lines.

You never want the bad actor to show up on the "set," i.e., of your life but you might not ever see that side of you. You could be totally oblivious of your bad actor self. Others will avoid your company because you become unpredictable and difficult to be around. However, if your bad behaviors, your bad attitudes, and your bad ideas show up, are you ready to investigate and address your distorted thinking? The check-in is crucial so that any inconsistencies can be remedied. The mind is the villain in your story; it takes you to places and switches things up on you. Has your mind ever tricked you?

I would get this job and make $300. I needed rent money. My mind told me I still had money for one dime, a drink, some cigarettes... but 2 hours later I had spent all the money. My mind convinced me as I was buying the crack that I was going to sell some of it. Well, you cannot ask the monkey to sell some bananas for you. I was so badly mangled. My mind was running off of that. I tried to think positively, but it would not work. When I was under the influence of my own mind, it became the villain of my story.

Albert Einstein said, "We cannot solve our problems with the same thinking we used when we created them."

Our ideas, emotions, and attitudes dominate all of us. When you feel shame, anger, resentment, fear, and doubt...., you are charged with those negative energies. Your emotions and perceptions are disfigured. You might cry when people are laughing, you might laugh when people are crying. You have some messed up ideas because your emotions are being charged by the wounds. You are a royal mess. You want a better life, but what you need is a better relationship with your mind and with yourself.

Every great story has an antagonist, someone who challenges the protagonist. This not only makes the story more exciting but provides the impetus for movement and the protagonist's transformation. Likewise, if we did not face challenges, we would not grow as much. We would become lazy, fat, and bored if never challenged or if we did not have to work very hard for the things we want. Our self-esteem would not be as high, and we would actually crave a challenge to prove ourselves. If we felt like we never earned anything, the only thing that would grow would be our discontentment.

> *I was never very good at math, and I needed to pass the big last test of my senior year. I decided the best thing to do was to cheat. I got an A on the test, and I did not get caught. I felt so good at first, even took in all the compliments from my teacher. I never felt any regret, my plan worked, or so I thought. But a strange thing started happening. Every year at my class reunion, my teacher would single me out and tell the story to inspire all the other students. I began to dread the story about me, each year got more and more challenging to hear it. I started feeling terrible about what I had done, and I finally had to tell my teacher the truth.*

The problem is that many of us feel that the villain has taken over our lives, that there is no hope to overcome it and succeed. We think that the world is stacked against us, and it is not a fair fight anymore. We become disillusioned with the ideas presented to us and disenfranchised with the system running it. Everyone else seems to have the magic bullet to make life work for them. How can some people thrive, while others struggle with their inner demons, and there is an internal battle they can never get under control?

Even though the mind is the villain, it does have magical abilities too. We know that expectations change our experience. There is little doubt that the placebo effect is a powerful component of whether we heal or not. One of the most powerful influences on our health is our attitude, beliefs, and thoughts around the healing. In every study testing the efficacy of a drug, there is a control group who takes a placebo. In every case, some people get better by just taking a placebo. How is this possible? There are no healing components within a placebo, it is inert.

A quote from one study explains, "We view the placebo effect as the product of your body's ability to heal, which is activated by our mindsets and expectations to heal, and shaped by medical ritual, branding of drugs and the words doctors say."

Most of us know about the placebo; however, we forget that the placebo effect remains in everything we do. It is the support system for it all. Your mindset is powerful; your perception affects the outcome. For example, if the test subjects believed it enough, it became real. The perceived benefits of anything that we are consuming or doing affect the outcome. The placebo subjects even produced specific neurobiological benefits in the brain. This is how they were able to harness the magic of the mind.

The real culprit is not the drink, not the crack pipe, not the food, not the sugar, not the gambling, not sex, not pornography, and not your social media. Our worst opponent is not outside of ourselves; it is inside of us, and it is the brain. Carl Jung noted this with many of his patients who proved difficult to heal. He said, "You have the mind of a chronic alcoholic." This is when you never seem to grow past the self-centeredness of a child. It is when you cannot find the self-sufficiency that others do. You cannot self-sooth your discontent, to quickly meet your needs without depending upon others.

Contentment and fulfillment are elusive, never within your reach. Your wants and needs become demands on others. If you become disappointed and hurt, now you have resentment, anger, and fear which will dominate your every move. Resentment, anger, and fear are the way we react when people, places, and things do not live up to our expectations. Resentment is how we deal with the past, always playing out the same stories and the same injustice. Anger is how we deal with the present moment, trying our best to get what we want when we want it, and right now. Fear becomes our modus operandi for the future, always afraid of the unknown and never feeling supported by anyone.

There is a reason you are drawn to drink or drugs or food, shopping, sex, gambling, or whatever your drug of choice is. It could be video games, but the effect is the same. The pleasure factors increase in the brain, and you numb the negative feelings from your life. This is why certain substances become addictive, they create increased levels of dopamine in the brain. It feels good. Give me more and more of it. Who does not want to feel good? No one. We all want to feel good most, if not all of the time.

But the problem is that it becomes a bottomless pit we are trying to fill up. Always trying to fill up the hole with something that makes us feel good. We are unable to sustain the good feeling for very long. We need more and more of whatever we can find, that elusive thing to boost us up. But sometimes the drop in our energy after the good feeling goes away feels worse than when we started. After a while, it starts to interfere with our daily activities, and our lives become unmanageable. Ask yourself, "Why do I have to feel good all the time?"

I loved to shop and buy new clothes, new shoes, new purses, whatever. I would like the new things for about a month, but then the feeling would wear off. I would go out and shop some more, with the same effect. At first, I would feel so great wearing new clothes to work. So, I kept up this way of life for many years, going into debt and eventually filing bankruptcy. I justified and rationalized it all, never believing that I was the problem. I blamed my debt on the fact that I did not make enough money!

We often tell ourselves that if we had so much money, then we would be happy. If I had a particular job, then I would be satisfied. If only I had a great relationship, then I would be happy. If I had that car, then I would be happy. If I had a fantastic wardrobe and could buy anything I wanted, then I would be satisfied. If I had a million dollars in the bank, then I would be happy. When I get out of debt, then I will be happy. All of that is just an illusion. It is a trick of the mind. The goal post keeps moving down the field, and we keep telling ourselves cover stories until we ask ourselves the right questions.

There is something much deeper going on within when you crave things to fill you up, to make you feel good about yourself. There is something much deeper going on when you crave things that will suppress your bad feelings. When you like things a little too much, there is a problem going on within. Generally, it is not a problem to like to gamble, but if you like it a bit too much, it becomes an issue. It is not a problem to enjoy a drink now and then, but if you like it too much where it becomes a necessity, and/or you have rationalizations and justifications of why it is not a problem, look deeper. It is not what you do, it is how you do it.

Any addiction is an obsessive-compulsive thought disorder. What this means is that if you stop the substance, your mind will start working on overdrive to keep you using. Doesn't matter if it is shopping, drinking, social media, or sugar. Your mind starts obsessing on the substance; it is compulsive, and you feel that you have no control over your thoughts. Most often, you will choose the old pattern of behavior to quiet the monkey brain. It gives you temporary relief until you need the 'fix' again. It becomes a vicious cycle, you become trapped, but you don't know it. Even if you give up one obsession, it is too easy to substitute it for another. That does not solve anything.

> I was so proud of myself for giving up hard drugs. I could boast and feel good about myself. Others in my support group were proud of me too. They clapped when I told stories about drinking and hitting my girlfriend when I said, "But at least I did not use!" It took me a long time to realize that I still had a lot of work to do. My mind was being so clever, but I had just substituted one thing for another. The evidence was showing up, but I kept denying its existence. My life was still unmanageable.

The brain is comprised of a conscious mind and a subconscious mind. The conscious mind communicates to the outside world and us through thought, speech, writing, and pictures. The conscious mind contains thoughts and beliefs that we are aware of. It is the part of our brain that analyzes, problem solves, rationalizes, and might even be creative. Numerous cognitive neuroscientists surmise that we use this part of our brain (our decisions, actions, emotions) about 5 to 10% of the time.

The subconscious part of our brain is mostly hidden from us. So most of our decisions, actions, emotions, and behavior depends on the 90 to 95% of our mind that we are not aware of. Things that the conscious mind wants to keep hidden from our awareness are stored into the unconscious. Even though we are not mindful of what is stored in our unconscious mind, it has a significant effect on our lives. Studies reveal that the subconscious mind is far more active, purposeful, and independent than previously thought. They are finding that we have these unconscious behavioral 'guidance systems' that are continually furnishing suggestions throughout the day about what to do next, and we often act on those signals without any conscious awareness. That is why some people's behavior might be so mystifying and unpredictable.

Dr. Carl Jung believed that we have the drive to achieve psychological independence from our parents, to cultivate a social life, to contribute to our community, to find a purpose, and eventually to face up to death. He believed it was inherent within all of us regardless of class or culture. But he also saw within the human race a tendency towards inertia, laziness or even self-sabotage. He said, "We are addicted to absolute laziness until circumstances prod us into action." He felt these guidelines (if we were capable) would lead to healthy development in life.

He also felt that if we allowed our fear and laziness to interfere with these life tasks, then they would become a chain around our necks. He labeled the unwilling as the neurotic who walked among the willing. This is the person who adopts a faulty attitude toward these tasks that we each long to do. He noted that the primary obstacle was the person's attitude toward them, not necessarily the tasks themselves. Usually, the obstacles are not insurmountable, but instead, it is the mind that creates the biggest challenge to succeeding.

Healthy people accept life's challenges and adapt their thinking and their behaviors to push through any challenge they are met with. No one is immune to difficult situations, but healthy individuals have resiliency and resolve no matter what life throws on their path. The neurotic individual does not admit their inadequacies, but instead deceives themselves and blames the obstacle.

Jung noted that the neurotic draws back from his life's tasks not because of any real impossibility to achieve them, but rather from an artificial barrier created by himself. From this moment on, he suffers from an internal conflict. Now the realization of his cowardice is apparent, and defiance and pride can take over. The individual has this inner conflict of push and pull, but inertia sets in. He is unable to take on any new enterprises until the conflict is resolved. "His efficiency is reduced, he is not fully adapted, he has become in a word – neurotic."

Jung theorized that if we do not continue to grow and achieve these tasks in life, we not only become stagnant, but we regress to more infantile modes of adaption. He believed that this regression as the response to the conflict is what generates the various symptoms of the neurosis. This could take the form of pervasive anxiety, phobias, obsessive-compulsive behaviors, depression, apathy, or obsessive and intrusive thoughts.

But these indications and warning signs can be used to alert us that a change is necessary for our lives. That by continuing with these same patterns can only get us the same results. Jung said, "There will be a tendency to retreat from life, and this will lead to regression in maturity, and this will, in turn, lead to more resistance from life." Jung did not see a single cause for the attitude toward life and the inability to adapt and mature. He saw each case as individual, for some, the blame lies with their genes, for others a poor upbringing, and for most, he saw a combination of genetic and environment. He believed that the best way to treat anyone was to bring a new way of thinking and help them adopt a new attitude toward life.

Oscar Wilde said you could tell a lot about a man if you put a mask on him. How would you act with a mask on? Would there be consistency or integrity to your behavior? Or are you one of those people who send out nasty anonymous messages via the internet? If you watch the film Groundhog Day, there is a moment when Bill Murray starts to become authentic, when he starts acting from principles and not from his personality or wounds. It was the only way he could transform his situation, and this set him free. It is an excellent metaphor for our lives too.

Investigate whether you are the same person behind closed doors or out in public. Is there a public persona and then a private persona? Which one is the authentic one? Probably neither one of them. Are you the same person with all your friends and associates or do certain groups only know certain things about you? This is a form of compartmentalizing your life. Why do you feel you cannot be yourself with any and all of your friends or co-workers? If there are secrets you cannot share with others, you are not living an authentic life. It takes considerable awareness to live consciously in the present moment.

Our unconscious mind does take over for most of our routine behaviors like brushing our teeth, getting dressed, eating, or driving to work. That works for the most part so that we can give our conscious brain a little rest and still get things done. But where it does not work is when we are trying to monitor ourselves throughout the day. We cannot zone out and hope it all works out, and we show up as authentic. If we are unaware of who showed up on the set, how can we possibly address the inconsistencies and the wounded child who showed up?

Most of your wounds and traumas occurred in your childhood. Because you were unaware of these wounds, they festered and became more and more infected and deeper and more difficult to heal because of all the time that has elapsed. If you were wounded at age four, the four-year-old shows up in stressful situations. If you were wounded in your teens, that teen is the one showing up in your marriage right now. The emotional wound stunts healthy, emotional growth, and the child will show up with some sort of a temper tantrum. The child is selfish, self-centered, and self-seeking.

It is not your fault what happened to you, but it is your responsibility to uncover your wounds and start the healing process. You know what happens if you do not take care of an external wound. The longer you wait, the worse it gets. Internal wounds need to be healed too. It might take longer for the outward manifestation of that "infection" to manifest, but it will show up in either your physical body and/or your disruptive emotional behavior. You can hide it for only so long, and then it becomes excruciatingly more and more difficult.

Just as the placebo effect is very powerful, the opposite, or the nocebo effect works just as effectively. Negative thoughts are just as powerful as positive thoughts. Whether we think we can, or we believe that we cannot, both can manifest as truth. If we believe that we are not good enough, it shows up in our lives. If our wounds are sending out negative beliefs, it will show up in our thoughts, words, and behaviors. Question the negative beliefs and never believe anything that is limiting you!

There are countless stories and example of people achieving the "impossible." Stories of people walking on hot coals, bending spoons, lifting cars off their loved ones, or even healing themselves. The mind is very powerful, and when we learn how to best harness it for our ultimate growth and emotional healing, we are living in the present moment and taking our power back. We take our power back when we stop being victims and start seeing how anything and everything can eventually make us stronger.

There is a children's book titled, *The Frog's Race,* by Dulce Rodrigues, that best illustrates this point. The story explains how one day, a group of frogs decided to make a race to see who would get to the top of a high tower. A lot of people came to watch the race and to give them support. But as soon as the race began, everyone started saying negative things like, "You will never make it!" "Give up now!" It does not make sense to keep trying!" One by one, the frogs felt discouraged and started falling out of the race. All but one little frog who kept pushing and pushing to the top. Deeply astonished, everyone wanted to know how she had managed to keep going despite all the yelling and shouts of disapproval. When they asked her, they realized that she was deaf! She thought everyone was encouraging her to finish, so she kept going until she won.

We are much like the frog in this story. We are often pulled off track by our own negative beliefs or the discouraging comments from others. If we are walking around in an unconscious state unaware of our own negative self-talk, we are never going to fulfill our dreams and purpose in life. However. being unconscious and blaming others for our so-called failed life is taking the easy way out.

The choice is yours, but it does take more effort to live from the conscious mind, being aware of ourselves in all aspects, good/bad, beautiful/ugly, light/dark, or conscious/ unconscious. This is the path to freedom, from the endless up and downs and from trying to fill ourselves up with superficial things that do not last. Remember the light is always there within you, you just need to uncover the darkness to reveal it. Your authentic self is there within you, the part of you that is most connected to the pure Source Energy of the universe. The limitless you!

Be aware of self-pity, defensiveness, loss of daily structure, lack of personal care, inability to set and maintain limits, indecision, compulsive behaviors, resentments, tendency to control people, situations, and things, blaming others, living in fear, a loss of belief in a higher power or yourself, a mind that feels out of control, mood swings, feeling powerless or lonely, and not being able to maintain proper support systems.

Be especially aware of what triggers you into a reactive state of mind. Try never to be hungry, tired, or under too much stress. These are natural triggers for most people. Watch the people you hang around with, are they uplifting you or draining you? Do your words and actions match? Are you consistent? Does the child show up to the set? Have you become a bad actor on a bad day in Bedrock?

WHEN WAS I REACTIVE THIS PAST WEEK OR MONTH?

WHAT CAUSED ME TO REACT BADLY?

WHAT WERE THE TRIGGERS THAT I IGNORED?

HOW DID I FEEL JUST BEFORE I REACTED BADLY TO ANOTHER?

WHEN AS A CHILD DID I FEEL THAT SAME FEELING?

HOW OFTEN DO I FEEL THOSE SAME FEELINGS AS AN ADULT?

WHAT LIMITING BELIEF DO I HAVE AROUND THIS FEELING?

IS IT TRUE?

HOW CAN I BETTER TAKE CARE OF MYSELF BEFORE REACTING BADLY?

CHAPTER NINE

Are You Ready For Your Close-Up?

After all, the prep work is done, and the cameras are in their place, the actors have makeup applied to get ready for their scene. There was a lot of work done behind the scenes to get to this place in production. It is imperative to be fully prepared when the lights are turned on, and the director calls, "Action!" The camera can detect if you are not being authentic, especially when it is time for your close-up. Can you tell if you are ready to be authentic in all aspects of your life? Are you ready for your close-up?

This chapter is dedicated to examining all the indicators and evidence of being authentic. It will help uncover the conflicts between your thoughts, feelings, beliefs, actions, and habits. If there is any inconsistency in the flow from your thoughts down to your behaviors or habits, it will reveal itself to you and others. There needs to be a level of transparency in your life before you can change and transform. If your thoughts are primarily negative, you can only create negative behaviors and habits.

Your **Thoughts** create **Feelings** create **Beliefs** create **Behaviors** create **Habits**

Any good story has many conflicts in it to create more drama and more challenges before achieving the end goal. If a story does not have any conflicts in it, it becomes tedious and boring. We might think, what is the point of telling this story? If a story has no conflicts, it would probably end reasonably quickly too. Stories are more exciting and engaging when they have twists and turns, both outside conflicts and internal conflicts within the actors.

Our external conflicts are obstacles along the journey, like losing our job, or the car breaking down. The internal conflicts might be not believing in ourselves, believing that cheating and stealing will solve all our problems, or being afraid of dying, just to name a few. We see in films how the protagonist's obstacles make achieving their end goal more and more difficult. Every time we have an obstacle in our lives, it will slow us down until we persevere through it.

Good drama in a film or television show is excellent. Too much drama in our daily lives is not a good thing, and it can actually become addictive. It can start to feel normal to have a lot of drama in that when it goes away, you will create some more. Life will feel boring if you don't have a fire to put out, someone to complain about, or a new victim story to gather sympathy from. We get a lot of attention from the dramas that play out in our lives. It also distracts us from dealing with our issues and shortcomings. Drama blocks our spiritual growth.

Drama creates an opening for your cover story to emerge. But the cover story has nothing to do with reality. It is a clever smokescreen that does not allow the person to examine the facts in front of him. The clever mind tells the person something other than the truth. The mind is playing tricks, and you never question yourself enough. It is only when there is a crisis that the cover story falls apart. The crisis has a way of showing you the truth.

I always told myself that I did not need anyone else and that I wanted to be completely independent. But I would also become hurt and disillusioned when my relationships did not work out. I felt like a part of me died when the relationship turned sour. It was so disappointing to me. I never questioned the discrepancy between what I was saying and what I was doing. The truth was that I did need others; I did want to become interdependent in a relationship. It was impossible to truly connect and let myself be vulnerable when I also wanted to be independent. I finally realized that my cover story did not work; that I wanted a great relationship. I also realized my cover story came about because of my pain of growing up without feeling like I had dependable caregivers. I could never depend on them, so I was going to show the world I was never going to depend on others!

If you choose to ignore your wounds and traumas for years and years, continually stuffing all the bad things off to the side to deal with them "later," your life will eventually become unmanageable. It might start with panic attacks with no origin or physical ailments such as horrible digestion or headaches. It might be that you begin feeling so uncomfortable around other people, or that you start having obsessive-compulsive thoughts of worry. This is the point where most people try to self-medicate to sooth the pain and mind. It is understandable, but it will lead to more and more unmanageability in your life. And then your habits become addictions.

Remember, the greatest story ever told is told by addicts. We always tell ourselves something that keeps us in the condition of addiction. We always tell ourselves that 'this is my life,' 'I know what I am doing,' 'I don't want anyone telling me anything,' or something that creates more isolation and delusion. However, there is always a contradiction in the story, and you are living another way than what is being told. The greatest lie becomes one you are telling yourself.

I was receiving public assistance, and I would wait for the check to come on a particular day. The idea that it was 'free money' kept me trapped in not looking for a real job. I told myself that I did not have to work so hard, but the reality was that I ended up working twice as hard during the month to hustle jobs to make ends meet. The 'free money' was not free at all. In fact, it was enslaving me not to reach my potential or to be productive. My mind was tricking me into believing that a job would trap me. But the reality was that I was set free when I finally broke the cycle and started working a job with a time clock.

Because our habits reside in our subconscious mind, for the most part, it takes a powerful examination to uncover the inconsistencies. Our mind can be very clever and can easily trick us if we are not willing to ask the right questions and be brutally honest with ourselves. If we choose to run our lives on auto-pilot, we will never get to the truth of the matter.

The sad part is that we can operate and function for most of the day on auto-pilot. We can cook breakfast, eat, shower, brush our teeth, get dressed, and drive to work without being fully present. We can do our job, drive home, eat and sit in front of the television without being fully in the here and now. This seems to work for a good many people, but it will not help you to break bad habits or to get in touch with who you really are. The real you is under all the garbage that has been piled onto you by your society, your culture, your family, your schools, your friends, your church, and even your 'enemies.'

What is the best indicator if you are living the life you profess to? What are your words and behaviors like when you are under stress?

What are you like when you feel squeezed by life? If you say you are not a racist, but then you get angry at a person of another race, do you call them derogatory names behind their back? Then you are a racist. You have some deep-seated beliefs held in your subconscious at the same time that you protest, "I am not a racist!" Do you claim to be a "moral" person but have no problems supporting people in politics or business who cheat, lie, steal, or commit other immoral acts? Then you are not a moral individual.

You have all these indicators that are giving you signs, but you don't listen or see them. You live out of your cover story, whatever it might be. You don't address the discomfort in your life, it is always someone else's fault. You keep moving the goal post down the field of what is OK or not OK, of what is acceptable or not. This helps you to be in denial when your life is out of control. You tell yourself that as long as I am not in prison, everything is fine. You could be controlling and threatening in your relationship, but as long as you are not using or breaking the law, you don't think you have to address how your life has become unhealthy or unmanageable.

You want everyone to think that your life is together, and you talk a good talk. But it just keeps you from digging deeper into telling yourself the truth of the matter. You can never be totally free from the cover story until you are willing to examine every aspect of your life truthfully. If there is any part of rationalization or justification or an "at least, I did not do this," your cover story is at play. You might not be able to see it, but others can. Have others tried to break your cognitive dissonance or your resistance to the truth? Were you open to hearing them?

Let's examine your thoughts first. Throughout the day, are most of your thoughts negative or positive? If you have no clue, start by paying attention to this detail by checking in every hour. Make a note of what ideas and thoughts keep running through your head. Is there negative self- talk like, 'I am not good enough,' 'I can't do that,' 'I am so stupid,' or 'I am fat and ugly'? We all have some degree of negative thoughts that run through our heads every day, so if you think that you have none, keep examining and be brutally honest. It's OK if you have negative thoughts; you are not a bad person if you do.

Now that you have examined some of the negative self-talk, how are those thoughts running your life? Are you not creating or acting upon opportunities because your thoughts talk you out of it before you even begin? Talk like, 'Why bother, I am too old to start that now.' Are you amazed at how negative your thoughts really are? Do you see that trying to get positive results from negative thoughts is much more difficult, if not impossible? You will never be able to get rid of all your negative thoughts, but you can quiet many of them when you start bringing them into your awareness.

Do your feelings align with your thoughts? If you have ideas about the futility of life, do you ignore your feelings and only show a happy face? Do you say you are confident, but underneath feel insecure and unsure about yourself? Are you angry at the world, but appear happy-go-lucky? Do you have a lot of shame about your past but never acknowledge it to others? Do you tell some people your dad is your hero, but tell others that you hate him because he abused you? Are you able to be vulnerable with those close to you; ready to share your fears and insecurities? Would others be shocked at how you really think and feel?

Your **Thoughts** create **Feelings** create **Beliefs** create **Behaviors** create **Habits**

A good indicator that you are living an authentic life is that your habits are in alignment with your beliefs. Look to your habits, for they will reveal what is going on deep inside of you. Do you say that you are confident, but you tend to shrink and play small when you are around others? Do you seldom feel comfortable speaking your truth to others? Do you come home and turn on the television rather than seek the connection and relationship you say you want? Do you say that you love yourself, but do your eating habits support that story? This is the way to uncover the real truth of your life. If there is a conflict between what you desire and how you see yourself, and the reality of what is truly happening, you have significant conflicts in your cover story.

Your perceptions can rob you, making you reactionary, and creating superficial drama. You find yourself getting in trouble with your reactions, and now you are off to the races and finding it hard to get out of the chaos you have created. You are caught in a reaction about what you think is true or right. But your thoughts could be corrupted, and this causes even more reactions. Making decisions based on desire could be disastrous. These desires could be based on an unhealthy model.

What are you using to define your bliss? Shopping, gambling, sex, drinking, drugs, or even social media? It might start out in a balanced way but quickly move into an obsession and overindulgence. The obsession creates a feeling of wanting to return to the place of bliss. Inside of the obsessions are justifications and rationalizations. I should have a drink. I deserve the extra cake. I need to go shopping! You can come up with all kinds of fantastic ideas to complete the task. But obsessive thoughts reduce choice and any spiritual principle like honesty will get lost in that too.

How do you really feel about yourself? Do you expect others to treat you better than you treat yourself? Sometimes the worst offenses have been perpetrated upon us by ourselves! When you start conducting yourself with dignity and self-respect, you will begin to feel better about yourself. This will help build some self-esteem. When you feel inadequate or impoverished, you need something to pick yourself up, but that never works. It will only happen from the inside – out. When you start feeling your worth, you will start acting better.

Relapse starts when you let go of your integrity. It takes you right back into the danger zone. You are trying to save your face, but your ass is on fire! Warning sign: Am I feeling discontented? We must always investigate and research ourselves every day. Our habits run our lives. What might that look like? Cigarettes continuously tell you what to do. After your coffee, what do you want? Habits are continually communicating with you. A habit is a custom, a fixed practice, as opposed to choice, which is more than one option. Habits limit your options.

> I used to buy my cigarettes every day. But I got a new job, and I did not get paid every day. I had planned on continuing this habit of buying my cigarettes every day, but my boss switched up on me. I could not get my cigarettes, so I quit my job. Then he only paid me ½ of my money! That came out of my best thinking!

Recovery isn't just about the 12 steps. It is becoming aware of your life. What happens when you go unconscious? You cannot use what is available; no access granted to higher wisdom. You cannot thrive. Wouldn't it be better to be conscious? You can be defined by your traumas, or you can be transformed by them. Know your strengths, weaknesses, and limitations. When you start knowing yourself, your confidence returns. What makes you go bump in the night? What are the inconsistencies in your character? You don't really know yourself until you start seeing your value.

Why does AA suggest you live by principles versus personality? Personality tries to rearrange the facts, contaminating the crime scene. Your brain is the most significant crime scene. Your mind will rationalize and try to minimize any success that you have. It will always limit an experience while it tries to make sense of things. Principles will not switch up on you. Honesty is being truthful; it is not about alternative facts or the grey areas that your clever mind will attempt to justify. Being honest is about having a great relationship with yourself.

I got tired of losing. I lost relationships, my mind, my money; I lost me! One day I stopped to take a look at my selfishness honestly. I did not like how that made me feel. Willingness is beautiful. It is a better direction for me, allowing for better experiences. I really got it one day when my Ex-girlfriend did not show up for me. She was always there for me. I felt it. I got it. I remembered how I had done that to so many people. It felt as if I was abandoned; it was so painful.

Sometimes it is the discomfort which will motivate us to do something different. Sometimes we just become tired of losing all the time. Sometimes we grow tired of all the drama and chaos around us. When we stop compromising ourselves to the indignation that our minds present to us, we are becoming healthy.

Your life will become more vibrant and more profound, the more you get to know yourself. Your acceptance of how things really are will be the fuel for your transformation. A clear indication that you have done the work is that feeling of peace and serenity surrounding you and also newfound confidence in yourself. There is a journey to finding one's authentic self. Start with the investigation.

1. Am I so prideful that I cannot hear another person's point of view?

2. Am I habitually lazy in my investigation of myself?

3. Are impulses leading my life?

4. Is my life unmanageable?

5. Do I have an excessive desire for wealth or possessions?

6. Do I feel discontent with my life?

7. Am I quick to anger thinking I have been insulted or injured?

8. Is there a lot of guilt, shame, or depression in my life?

9. Do I blame others for my life or circumstances?

10. Do I criticize myself and others a lot?

11. Am I self-destructive?

12. Is my makeup smeared with self-pity?

13. Do I always feel less than?

14. Am I still rationalizing and justifying many things?

15. Do I find myself trying to control and manipulate others?

16. Do I feel overwhelmed with life and go into fear?

17. Do I have a tendency to be unfocused with my head in the clouds?

18. Am I quick to anger, to lash out at others, and hold grudges?

Here are some indicators and evidence of living authentically.

1. Do I feel like I have a choice over most situations?

2. Am I at peace for most of the day?

3. Am I willing to take responsibility for my life?

4. When I feel criticized, can I not take it personally and hold my peace?

5. Am I able to hear another's pain and problem without trying to solve it for them?

6. Can I be an inspiration to help others and accept where they are on their path?

7. Can I find true meaning by being of service to others rather than being self-centered, self-seeking, or selfish?

8. Can I feel negative feelings without wanting to resist them?

9. Can I acknowledge when I just want to be right even at the expense of someone else?

10. Can I not hold anyone hostage because of how I feel?

11. Can I quickly say, "I don't know"?

12. Do I feel happy when others succeed?

13. Am I able to find my center quickly when I get pulled off balance?

14. Am I telling myself and others the truth even when it is difficult?

15. Do I feel grateful for most of the day?

It is only with an honest assessment that you can create the life that you desire!

JOURNAL

WHAT DOES CHOICE LOOK LIKE FOR ME TODAY?

DO I FEEL DISCONTENTED?

WHAT DOES ABSTINENCE LOOK LIKE IN MY LIFE?

HOW MUCH DRAMA DO I HAVE IN MY LIFE?

DO I MISTAKE PEACE FOR BOREDOM?

HOW MANY FIGHTS HAVE I BEEN IN THIS PAST MONTH?

ACKNOWLEDGMENTS AND APPRECIATION

Because sometimes you just need a little help along the way.

Matt Di Lorenzo
www.coherenthealing.com
Distance healing/clearing for the emotional body

Mas Sajady
www.mas-sajady.com
Workshops and meditations to clear lifetimes of patterns and programming

Drunvalo Melchizedek
www.theschoolofremembering.com
Meditation workshops to awaken the heart

Jon Sweeney
www.spiritwords.com
Distance healing and chi for physical body rejuvenation

Camille Moritz
www.heavenonearthjustforbeing.com
Intuitive guidance, past life clearings to help restore the magic of life

Special thanks to Dr. Fred Walker and Kayo Anderson for taking the time to read our manuscript and for giving us valuable feedback. Our book is better because of you!

Book Cover Art by Joan of Angels

 Joan of Angels is a visionary artist that can see, feel, and access beings in other dimensions which bring forth wisdom, energy, and guidance necessary for human development and ascension. Her paintings become infused with the frequency and energy of each unique insight and artistic expression.

She is an oracle who offers one-on-one soul awakening sessions or group events. These private or group sessions can help you align with your life purpose by focusing your energies toward living your fullest potential.

To book a private oracle reading or group events, kindly visit Joan at her website.

Her artwork is also available for purchase as original acrylics, giclée's, prints, cards, scarves, and shopping bags.

If you wish to commission a piece, contact Joan directly to discuss. Each purchase of original art includes a mini reading from Joan of Angels.

www.joanofangels.com

About the Authors:

Christopher Mack has been facilitating recovery groups in Los Angeles for the past 16 years. He has been interviewed many times (NPR, LA Times, USA Today, LA Weekly, and Nightline) because he has a unique perspective about the condition of homelessness and our human nature. He is a beloved fixture on Skid Row in downtown Los Angeles, having worked for JWCH as an outreach worker for many years. He is known to many as The Urban Sage. Because Christopher used music and singing to uplift himself from the daily tribulations, he co-founded The Urban Voices Project five years ago, a choir for the urban community and underserved population.

Wanda Webster graduated from Drake University with a bachelor's degree in Special Education and Psychology. When she moved to Los Angeles, she accepted opportunities in the entertainment industry working as a development executive and a literary agent. She discovered she had a natural gift at helping writers develop and fine-tune their scripts. Many of her writers won awards in their field. More recently, Wanda obtained a master's degree in Education and Psychology from Pepperdine University. She created curricula for large non-profits in the areas of spirituality, social-emotional development, and addiction/recovery. Wanda has always been fascinated by human behavior and believes that supporting people to become the best versions of themselves to be her ultimate joy and purpose.

CPSIA information can be obtained
at www.ICGtesting.com
Printed in the USA
FSHW022001190919
62206FS